# Be the Light!

*How Positive Projection Builds
and Inspires an Extraordinary Workplace!*

**Darryl Ross**

Copyright © 2020

All Rights Reserved

ISBN: 9798669459963

# Dedication

*For I know the plans I have for you," declares the Lord, "plans to prosper you and not to harm you, plans to give you hope and a future. Jeremiah 29:11*

*To Jennifer Ross. My super wife, Mom, best friend, and love, this book couldn't have happened without you. And to our awesome kids Javon and Jazmine. I love you, dearly. You inspire me every day!*

# Table of Contents

POSITIVE PRAISE ................................................................. I

INTRODUCTION ................................................................. 1

CHAPTER 1: THE POWER OF COMPASSION & KINDNESS ............... 6

CHAPTER 2: CREATING GUEST EXCELLENCE ..................... 17

CHAPTER 3: MANAGING THE MESSAGE ........................ 29

CHAPTER 4: THE FOUNDATION OF LEADERSHIP ............................ 41

CHAPTER 5: EMPOWERING THE TEAM ............................. 53

CHAPTER 6: LEAN INTO CONFLICT .................................... 66

CHAPTER 7: THE CHARACTER OF RESILIENCE ............................. 78

CHAPTER 8: OUR DIFFERENCES MAKE THE DIFFERENCE .............. 91

CHAPTER 9: IT'S A MATTER OF TRUST ......................................... 103

CHAPTER 10: THE LIGHT OF PURPOSE ................................. 113

# Positive Praise

I have seen many motivational speakers in the business world over the last 30 years, and Darryl's presentation and flow were by far the BEST, I have been too. I loved his energy and passion, and it was a refreshing look at change. My main takeaway was BE THE LIGHT! Keep up the great work! -*Scott Johnson, Director* **Motorola**

Darryl Ross was amazing. He was engaging, energetic, and entertaining. He really was intuitive with the Tampa Bay Way. He did his research of our company to ensure he presented what we were asking for. Before the event, he contacted us several times and returned any communication we sent promptly. Our team loved him and would recommend him for any event you may have. - *Amber McGee, Human Resources* **Tampa Bay Federal Credit Union**

All I can say is WOW!! We loved, loved, loved Darryl! Great points, loved the videos, and so many take-aways that the attendees can start using now. Thank you so much! We are so excited to have you back with us in Grand Rapids in August! *-Andrea Starmer, Education Specialist* **COVERYS**

Darryl was great and received all positive feedback from our conference. What struck me mainly was the time he took to "personalize" his session to specifically relate to our organization and attendees, rather than just presenting a "cookie-cutter" keynote. He was a joy to work with professional, warm, and extremely accommodating. I look forward to working with Darryl again shortly! *- Marian Desilets, Conference Chair & Board Administrator* **Association of Registration Management**

I highly recommend Darryl Ross. His preparation for the event was unparalleled, and it showed in his speech. Darryl is a mix of motivational speaking and business training, wrapped in a dynamic personality. Everyone was engaged throughout his time and has since inquired if we can have him present at future events. *-Cheryl Carr, Director of Marketing & Donor Relations* **KEDPLASMA**

Darryl was so passionate and a wonderful storyteller. He connected with the group and left us with many great messages, including "Be the light!" We've already received several requests to have him back. -*Jenifer Murphy, Manager of Patient Safety* **VCU Health**

First, I want to say including a speaker in our sales/operations kick-off meeting was a last-minute decision. I was amazed at how quickly Darryl understood our business and could tailor his presentation to both our industry and what the organization is currently experiencing. He was knowledgeable, energetic, and engaged everyone throughout the entire presentation. The session was two weeks ago, and employees are still talking about it and referencing some of the things we learned. We were beyond pleased and cannot wait to work with him again. -*Desiree T, Manager* **Dade County Federal Credit Union**

# Introduction

In 2010, I moved my family from Las Vegas, Nevada, to Severn, Maryland. My wife and I, two young children, and dog Bailey embarked on a cross-country road trip for five days. My fondest memory was driving through Oklahoma and Texas with no satellite radio and everyone in the car, including my dog Bailey, snoring loudly. The sound of their careless, fleeting snores was like music to my ears and brought content to my heart. I kept myself awake, eating Milk Duds, drinking Red Bull, and singing Barry Manilow tunes.

Finally, we made it to Maryland. We left our 2,000 square foot house, with a home office, a pool, Jacuzzi, friends, and a remarkable church behind in Nevada and moved into 850 square feet, two-bedroom apartment. Won't lie; it kind of hurt my pride. In Vegas, we had a doggy door off the side of the kitchen to our backyard for Bailey to come and go as he pleased. We never had to take him out, but now we had to. In Maryland, everything changed. The positive side of the D.C. area was a number of museums, monuments, and restaurants. The career lifestyle was comprised of corporate, military, and government professionals. The downside was that it was costly. The summers were hot and humid, with plenty of mosquitoes. In the winter, we endured plenty of cold, sleet, and some snow. The worst part was the traffic. Wow! I used to tell people, "In the D.C. area, you'll wait in traffic to get to the real traffic!" Some people say there are four seasons. I disagree. There are only two main seasons - winter and road repair.

After living in Maryland for about two weeks, my wife stopped me on my way out the door and yelled, "I'm not happy here!" It was six in the morning. My car was literally running outside, and I was rushing to go to work, yet I stopped to ask her what's wrong. She said, "People aren't friendly here. No one says hello in the grocery store; no one waves from across the parking lot, no one holds the door and smiles at the bank, I'm not happy here!"

Again, since I was rushing to go to work, I thought of something quickly to say and said, "Well, honey, you *be the light*. I'll do it too. Why don't we decide as a family that we're going to be the light? We'll be the ones to wave in the parking lot; we'll be the ones to say good morning; we'll be the ones to hold the door at the bank. Why don't we just decide as a family to be the light?"

My wife thought about it for a minute and then said, "We are the new people; they should be nice to us!"

I had to admit; she had a point. But we did it anyway, and something special occurred. It stuck. We still say, "Be the Light." Five years later, we moved to Winter Garden, Florida. Our son was going to third grade, and our daughter was starting kindergarten. This was a difficult transition, because we were finally comfortable in the D.C. area, and felt connected. This move would require an adjustment, making new friends, and the kids attending a new school.

Back in Maryland, we had started saying prayers as a family to start the day and continued this tradition in Florida. We would stand in the kitchen in a circle holding hands, and I would typically lead us in prayer for all of us to have a good day and for our safety. "Amen." Then I would say, "Be the Light." Jennifer, my wife, would gracefully say, "Be the Light." Our daughter, Jazmine, would yell very exuberantly, "Be the Light!"

Then, my son, Javon, would painfully and grudgingly grumble, "Be the Light," because he was in third grade and trying to be cool. But then, something amazing happened. That year, the school superlative awards came out, and my son won two awards. He won *Best Reader*, which was great to hear as a dad. He also won *Kindest Kid,* voted by his fellow students. Absolutely amazing! I realized for the first time that he was buying into our little ritual and saw it daily as an example. So, *Being the Light* made sense to him.

You might think this is just a story about a child…it's not! This is a story about people. Being the light focuses our energy on positive projection. It is all about shining our personal light outward. Yes, to our family, but also to our boss, our co-workers, and definitely our customers too. How different would the culture of your organization be if everyone practiced positive projection, every single day? This book will highlight many areas in the workplace where we can win the day with positivity and use our talents and gifts to make a bigger impact, while also shining our positive projection on others so we can absolutely. **Be the Light!**

*Be kind; for everyone
you meet is fighting a hard battle.*

**-*Plato***

# Chapter 1
# The Power
# of Compassion & Kindness

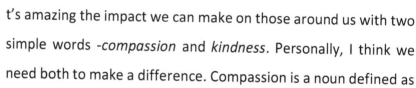

It's amazing the impact we can make on those around us with two simple words -*compassion* and *kindness*. Personally, I think we need both to make a difference. Compassion is a noun defined as *'a heart-felt feeling where you feel the sorrow of another person and sympathize with them. This urges you to do something substantial to remove their misery.'* Kindness is a noun which can also be used as a verb, defined as *the state of being kind*. Kindness is the quality of being friendly, generous, and considerate.

Compassion is more of a feeling we have, and it is very important that we connect with that level of emotion. However, kindness is an action. We actually have to do something in kindness. For kindness to be effective, you need to say kind words, be generous, and be helpful. This makes kindness a demonstration of our compassion. To begin this book, I would like to share a very significant experience in my life that highlights the power of compassion and kindness.

My wife Jennifer and I married on October 6, 2003. Since then, everything in our life was going great. We were living together in Las Vegas, Nevada, in our first home and had a baby golden retriever named Bailey. All of a sudden, something started nudging my wife on the shoulder. She felt that we had something we were missing in our perfect life. It was the presence of children. She wanted us to grow our family. I must admit, I was finally at the place where I was ready to embark on this special journey too.

Our daily lives changed drastically because of our new mission. Both of us invested our time and effort by making sure we were doing everything that was necessary and in the right way. Since it was taking much longer than we expected, we went from romantic intimacy to scheduling sex, to time it with her ovulation. It was my duty to go to CVS Pharmacy every week and buy more and more ovulation kits. That was always a little awkward. Every time I had to make the visit, I would quietly sneak through the pregnancy aisle to grab the ovulation kit and then head to the cashier. I would also throw in some Tic Tacs or Milk Duds to make my purchases look less obvious. The whole situation was ironic because we went from years trying to be careful not to get pregnant to actually trying to get pregnant.

Everything we did showed us how dedicated we were to become parents. Unfortunately, we were having challenges. We experienced three miscarriages in a row. According to medical studies, one-quarter of all pregnancies are likely to end in a miscarriage. Before week 12, 85% of estimated miscarriages happened. After a woman suffers a miscarriage, she typically goes through a procedure called dilation and curettage, known simply as a DNC. It's a surgical procedure, which removes the fetus and eliminates tissue from the uterus.

Jennifer had gone through these two times in the past 18 months, but this third time was different. I clearly remember being at the St. Rose Dominican Hospital. It was located in a suburb of Las Vegas in a town named Henderson. It was a relatively new hospital and opened in the year 2000. As soon as I walked in, there was a gift shop in true Las Vegas fashion. I saw extravagant gifts such as miniature Las Vegas hotels, key chains, caps, and teddy bears, wearing Las Vegas T-shirts. Only in the back were there some flowers.

As I went to check us in, there were wheelchairs stationed by the desk. I grabbed one for Jennifer. She was moving very slowly with short hurried steps, holding her stomach. Now one thing I can tell you about my wife is that she is tough. She has been a professional dancer for 15 years, graduating from the Royal Academy of Dance from

Ryerson University in Toronto. She knows her body very well and can manage physical pain. However, this third miscarriage had weakened her spirit. Although she was fighting the pain of the miscarriage, I think the emotional pain was much worse this time.

With tears in her eyes, she kept asking, *"Why? Why can't we have children? What's wrong with me? Other people seem to have kids despite the complications. Why can't we?"*

We were both devastated at this point. We just wanted to get the DNC over with and go home. After we waited for some time, the doctor came out to the lobby to speak with me before the procedure. Jennifer was the first patient that morning.

"She should be back very soon," the doctor said. On average, a DNC takes approximately 10 to 15 minutes, so I was already checking my watch for the time. "We are taking Jennifer back right now," the doctor said as I whispered a prayer in Jennifer's ears and watched as they rolled her into the surgery area.

It had been half an hour since Jennifer was inside. I said to myself, "It's okay. They're probably just wrapping things up." I tried to pass the time flipping through a magazine. Soon 45 minutes had passed. I was gradually starting to get concerned. I walked up to the front desk and asked the young lady behind the desk, "Excuse me, can you give me an update on Jennifer Ross, please? I'm her husband, Darryl Ross."

The front desk girl seemed to have no idea who I was. "Let me check," she said. She went to the backroom, came back, and said, "I'm sure they'll be out soon."

I was confused by her indifference, but I ignored it because of the state I was in. "Is there a problem?" I emphasized.

"Well, I couldn't go into the surgery area. I'm sure she'll be done soon," she said nonchalantly. That wasn't too reassuring, but I tried to relax.

It had been an hour now. I started pacing the hallway. I was confused. *Why is it taking so long?* No one came out to the lobby to give me an update. With each passing minute, my anxiety was going through the roof. This was where I started to panic. The doctor said the DNC should take 10-15 minutes and it had been 75 minutes now. *What on earth is going on?* I thought there must have been a complication, Jennifer was in trouble. I kept pacing, trying my best to keep my cool, but my heart rate was skyrocketing, and I couldn't stand it anymore.

"Where is my wife?" I yelled out loud. People started gathering around me. I was sure they were about to call security. Just in time, the doctor came out. She was immediately apologizing, trying to calm me down. I could barely breathe. "What's wrong? Is everything okay?" I asked.

The doctor gave me a look of apprehension then told me that my wife's cervix shut down, and she could not complete the DNC. They tried many times, but Jennifer's body went through what they call a shock trauma state. The doctor said that instead of going through her cervix, they tried to go through her abdomen, which left three large scars, but that didn't work either. At this point, the doctor had no choice but to admit her into the hospital for 48 hours. The doctor gave Jennifer a medication that would replicate the DNC, but at a much slower rate. The doctor told us the medication would take a couple of days to complete its cycle. Until then, they wanted us to stay in the hospital. We were given a room on the third floor directly across from the nurses' station. The only problem was the fact that the third floor of St. Rose Dominican Hospital was the labor and delivery floor. We were in shock. After a miscarriage and an unsuccessful DNC, we were assigned a room on the same floor, where all the labor and deliveries were taking place. It seemed like a cruel joke. All around us was the joy and pure excitement of babies being born. I clearly remember hearing and seeing families running down the hallways with flowers and balloons to visit their loved ones.

To make things worse, every time a baby was born, there was a hospital speaker just outside of our door that would ring chimes to announce the birth. We heard the echoes of those chimes all night long. I thought to myself, this seemed so unfair. It was bad enough that we suffered another miscarriage. But then we had to endure this. Slowly, I was moving past the emotional hurt of the miscarriage. I was angry that my wife was being forced to go through this situation. I was mad at the nurses, doctors, the hospital, and everyone I saw. For the night, I moved my chair closer to Jennifer's bed to give her a sense of comfort. We just stayed there, crying and praying for two days. On the evening of the second day, in walked Nurse Tracy. She was barely five-foot-tall, had blonde hair, wore glasses, and had an authoritative quality about her. She walked in and shockingly said, "What are you doing here?" Jennifer and I looked at her, very confused. Nurse Tracy quickly left the room, stomping the ground beneath her. We could hear the noise coming from the nurses' station and papers flying all over the place. She came back in abruptly. "Pack your bags. You're leaving," she instructed us. Before we knew it, Nurse Tracy moved us from the third floor to the fifth floor.

The fifth floor was the rehabilitation floor and had no labor and delivery sound system installed. Once settled in our room, the first thing Nurse Tracy did was apologize to us. "I'm so sorry. I'm sorry you suffered a miscarriage. And I'm especially sorry we had you stay on the third floor. They just didn't think when they roomed you. Please forgive us," she said.

Jennifer and I were speechless. It was the first time anyone at the hospital acknowledged the pain we went through. Nurse Tracy told us that she would be on duty all night. If there was anything we needed, she told us not to hesitate to call her. She also promised that she would brief the other nurses so everyone would be aware of our situation. This was a breakthrough moment for my wife and me. I could feel my anger begin to drain away. Nurse Tracy accompanied us for a while and asked us about our families and what our lifestyle was like living in Las Vegas. She seemed to care about us. As she was leaving, she said, "I can't promise you a baby. I wish that I could. But the good news is, you're conceiving. I know many couples that don't get that far." Then she teasingly told me, "Keep trying, big boy." That was the first time I laughed in days.

Much like the definition, Nurse Tracy had a deep feeling of sorrow and wanted to alleviate the suffering we were going through. But then she also backed it up with the action of kindness. She jumped on the phone, shifted some patients around, and moved Jennifer and me to a different room on a different floor. She understood the magnitude of having us stay on the third floor after a miscarriage. She went out of her way to accommodate us and kept us content.

The only downside of focusing on compassion and kindness is that it takes time. You need to listen actively and possibly take on some additional tasks to assist the patient or customer. However, the upside is that kindness doesn't cost more money. You don't need to hire extra staff. You don't need mandatory training or a company initiative. You just need to have the ability to empathize and understand that even though you can't fix everything, your compassion and kindness will produce a much healthier, happier, and compliant customer.

Years later, on March 21, 2007, Jennifer and I were back at St. Rose Dominican Hospital, but this time for a happy occasion. It was for the birth of our son, Javon Ross. Then we were back again on September 24, 2009, for the birth of our daughter, Jazmine Ross. The best part was we heard the chimes both times as the loudspeaker announced the births of our children. Jennifer and I searched the hospital for Nurse Tracy. When we found her, we hugged and thanked her for giving us her compassion and kindness during our hard time.

BE THE LIGHT!

Compassion is an essential part of our personal and professional lives. Nurse Tracy was the epitome of a professional in the workplace who used compassion and kindness. As an employee, what can you do to show more compassion and kindness?

- Being aware of and validating someone's hardship
- Being moved by another person's pain emotionally
- Wanting to alleviate the suffering from others
- Willing to take action and help others overcome obstacles

*Thank you...Nurse Tracy!*

> *"I have learned to imagine an invisible sign around each person's neck that says, make me feel important!"*
>
> **-Mary Kay Ash, Founder of Mary Kay Cosmetics**

# Chapter 2
## Creating Guest Excellence

To truly *be the light*, we must serve others. To keep it top of mind, just think back on the last time you experienced excellent customer service. Think about what made it great.

Was there a particular person who was attentive or friendly? Oftentimes, we don't know precisely what it was that made us experience excellent customer service. It is much like what Maya Angelou said: *"People will forget what you said, people will forget what you did, but people will never forget how you made them feel."*

When a business prioritizes its customer service to how customers feel, it creates guest excellence. At all times, we should have a target for these aspects when we serve our customers: hospitality, courtesy, positivity, and how you can exceed the expectations of the guest.

Ask yourself this question: Do you have an attitude of service? Do you believe customer service is part of your job, or do you think it's just an extra thing you have to do? Many organizations focus on their targets solely and put very little focus on customer service. To make up for it, they quickly roll out a customer service initiative where they focus on service for a particular week or month. But as you can imagine, things always go back to the true culture of their organization. If the culture of your organization is service-oriented, then putting extra focus on service training will only elevate guest excellence. However, if your organization follows a non-service culture, focusing primarily on money or bottom-line outcomes, then having a quick service training for a week or two will do very little to change the service culture of your organization.

To create guest excellence, all employees at your organization must understand that customer service is 100% part of their job and should be built into the DNA of the organization. The expectation should be for all employees to maintain a service-oriented culture.

In the early 1990s, I had the thrill of my life working as a performer and cruise staff member for Royal Caribbean Cruise Lines. My ship was called the MV Nordic Prince, and we primarily did seven-day cruises to the Eastern and Western Caribbean. As I was new to the position, I did not realize how competitive the cruise line industry was. Every week, we were ranked by the passenger comment cards and compared against other cruise ships' operating at that time. We would share with passengers how important it was that they fill out the comment card on the last day of the cruise. We could not coerce a positive comment. We could only ask the passenger for their participation in the survey. The comment cards gave the organization a real-time indication of how successful we were with customer service and the overall passenger experience. At that time, if you were hovering between 88% and 92% positive ratings, it was considered satisfactory, but unfortunately, we were consistently getting 84% approval.

I found myself in what I would like to call an *underachieving meeting*. This happened when the director called a meeting with all the staff and yelled at everyone. Using a power point presentation, the director explained how everything was going wrong and how we were not meeting our satisfaction numbers. In the room, there were about 50 cruise staff and managers from different departments.

During the meeting, the director was literally walking around the table and yelling, *"We've got to get to 88%! We've got to get to 88%! What are you going to do? What are you going to do? We've got to get to 88%!"*

I was very green and new to cruising and the whole passenger comment card challenge. So, I asked what I thought was a logical question, but it was quite obvious the seasoned veterans in the room thought I was crazy. I raised my hand and said, *"Is there a reason we can't be higher? Maybe 90%, 95%, even 100%?"* The room went cold. Everyone looked at me like I had two heads. They were obviously repulsed by my youthful exuberance and ignorance and just rolled their eyes at me. So, I slid back down in my chair.

When the meeting came to an end, a lady named Debra Krager walked up to me. It turned out that Debra was the new director who was going to take over and was silently participating in the meeting from the back of the room. She introduced herself to me and said, *"Kid, I like where your mind is at. But I don't like you blurting things out in the meeting,"* with a crooked smile. *"But you're right. I've been cruising for 20 years, and we've been hanging on to this 88% thing for all my 20 years. I'm putting you in charge. You're our new customer relations manager. However, you're not going to get any more money,"* she laughed. *"You can put it on your resume or something. But I want you to pick five people and go."*

I asked her what that meant.

She said, *"Go! Go out there and use your new young eyes to see what we can do better around here. I'll support you."*

So, off I went. I picked people with positive attitudes who loved our ship and thought that we could do better. After much discussion, we realized we had two major problems. First, the nature of cruising meant you are with the passengers for the entire week. If you had a negative experience with a passenger on day one, you would see them for six more days, and they probably wouldn't forget it. It was not like a restaurant where they'd leave at the end of the evening or even a quick weekend stint in a hotel. You were surrounded by the same passengers all week long. So, it was imperative that we made a strong first impression and continued that level of service for the rest of the week.

The second problem was that we were one of the smallest ships in the Royal Caribbean fleet. Our amenities for the passengers were quite meager. At that time, the flagship cruise liners were the Sovereign of the Seas and the Majesty of the Seas. Both of those ships were brand-new, twice our size, and with every amenity, you could think of. The MV Nordic Prince was older, smaller, and with very few bells and whistles. So, most of the cruise staff believed we could not do any better because our ship was not grand. However, my team and I thought we could use our small size and lack of amenities to our advantage. We thought we could make more of a personal connection with the passengers.

So, we set off to do just that. We wanted to commit to certain positive behaviors, always. So, the Service Sequence was born. The Service Sequence is not rocket science and somewhat common sense, but we realized quickly for our cruise ship that it was not common practice. Gradually, we trained the entire staff in the Service Sequence, which focuses on these four core behaviors.

## Eye Contact & Smile

We noticed that we barely made eye contact and rarely smiled at the passengers. Many of these families saved their money for years to be able to go on a cruise, and we treated them almost like they were a nuisance. Of course, this was back in the 1990s, but even today, with the infusion of handheld devices, it is our natural tendency to look down. We believed that eye contact and a great smile is almost a lost art. So, we made a commitment to making eye contact and smiling to every passenger, always.

## Warm Greeting

Shortly after eye contact and smile, it is necessary to provide a warm greeting. We found this to be one of our secret weapons. Since we did not have fantastic amenities for the passengers to run off to, this was our opportunity to learn a little bit about them. *"Welcome aboard the Nordic Prince! My name is Darryl. Where are you coming in from?"* The warm greeting typically led us to find out their name and where they were from. Then, we would tell them our name and where we were from. It was just like the beginning of a real conversation. Our little secret was to try and remember ten passengers' names (at a minimum). We would look for them throughout the week and say *Hello* and say their names out loud. The passengers were always amazed that we remembered their names.

## Active Listening

The art of *active listening* is an entryway to compassion. While you listen to someone, you can have your moment of introspection. This is a very important step because, typically, in human conversations, we are not very good listeners. We typically listen only to respond. While someone else is talking, we stay quiet long enough to jump in with our own comment, cutting them off midsentence or answering their question for them.

Instead, we wanted to listen to understand. When passengers came on board, they usually had many questions and were sometimes a little bit confused. It was our job to listen to them actively so we could address any questions they had or any concerns.

## Courteous Action Step

Finally, we would end the service sequence with a courteous action step. Meaning, *what's next for the passenger?* If we actively listened, we should know exactly what the passenger needs. We had to own that conversation with the passenger and be certain to be courteous and finalize the engagement. The next step might be that we get the passenger to a different department, maybe to the Purser's office or to make a reservation with the Maître D'. Maybe the next step was something we could take care of ourselves. Regardless, it was important that we take the next appropriate step, while being courteous.

## The Service Sequence Model

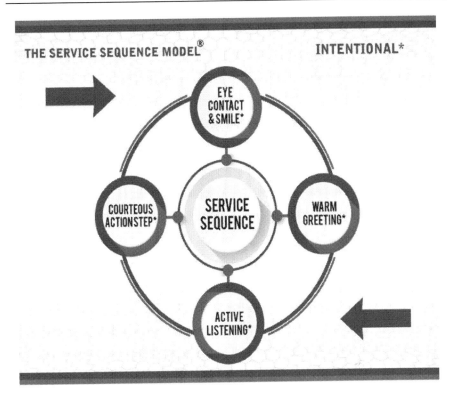

Slowly, we began to focus on all four behaviors consistently on every single 7-day cruise. It took a while to roll this out throughout the entire ship, but that was our goal. As the first few weeks of passenger comment cards came in, they did not seem to reflect our efforts. But we stayed diligent. Then all of a sudden, during the mid-second month, there was a shift. We went up a few percentage points, then the following week a few more, then the following week a few more. Word began to spread throughout the cruise staff.

Focusing on service and guest excellence became contagious as we consistently made gains week after week. Then the champagne moment arrived. We moved our positive passenger comment scores from 84% to 97.2% in just four months. For the first time, the passengers were actually using our names in the comment cards. It was amazing!

*Being the light* in service is not only leading your current team, but it is also an example of service to newly hired personnel. How can you be sure that your organization is creating guest excellence, from the moment a new employee is hired?

- During the interview process, candidates should be hearing and learning about the service culture. (Yes, that early!) As soon as your hiring manager meets a potential employee, service expectations should be discussed.
- Employees should experience guest excellence during their New Employee Orientation. In so many organizations, orientation is a wasted opportunity. You have hired a new employee and run them through paperwork and CBL's (Computer Based Learning) to get them up to speed. Then off they go reporting to their department. Although the paperwork and CBL trainings are important, organizations

should make time to discuss service expectations as well and set the tone for creating guest excellence.

- Finally, treat your employees the way you want them to treat the guests. Literally, your employees (in words and actions) should see guest excellence coming first from their manager or leader. We can talk about customer service or guest excellence all day long, but if leadership is not providing this to the employees, the employees will never provide it to the guests.

*"Whether you are big or small, you cannot give good customer service if your employees don't feel good about coming to work."*

*-Martin Oliver*

*The problem with communication is the illusion that it has taken place."*

***-George Bernard Shaw***

# Chapter 3
# Managing the Message

George Bernard Shaw's quote is one of my favorites of all time. I think it perfectly describes the challenge of communication. Many times, we say one thing, but the person on the receiving end hears something completely different. If that's true, then how can we manage communication in the workplace? *Being the light* at work means we are mindful of this challenge, and we seek opportunities for clarity in our communication. So, the question is, can we manage the message and be better communicators? The answer is *yes*.

I received my bachelor's degree from James Madison University in Harrisonburg, Virginia. I was always drawn to the psychology of communication and the interpersonal dynamics at work. My first introduction to the process of managing the message was during my freshman year in college. The course was called *Public Relations 101*.

My professor, Dr. Woal, was an elderly, unassuming man, but by far, my favorite instructor. He made us think through situations and problems with open classroom discussions. I will never forget the first day of class when he walked into the room and passed out a one question true-or-false test. This basically meant you received either an A or an F. That's it!

The question was: *The message sent is never the message received.* **True** or **False**

I looked at the question and thought, *Is this a trick?* We can't really say never about anything, can we? So, I circled *false* and turned my test in. In typical Dr. Woal fashion, he led an open discussion about the question over the remaining 90 minutes of class. The classroom discussed television commercials, political speeches, corporate statements, and even interpersonal communication between friends and loved ones. By the end of the discussion, I realized I was wrong.

Question: *The message sent is never the message received.* The answer is definitely **True**. Why?

Because even the most basic form of communication is constantly trying to reach its destination through countless communication barriers. For communication to be effective, there is a sender and a receiver. Everything in the middle of the message are the communication barriers. The question was created from a P.R. point of view. The theory goes that the message is never completely received by the consumer because of communication barriers that exist between them.

Let's use a typical television commercial as our example of receiving a message. During a commercial break, you see a 30-second commercial then it ends. Did you receive the message it intended to deliver? Probably not, because of barriers. In this situation, the communication barriers could have been the environment around you; maybe you were not able to hear or see the commercial properly. Another barrier could be that someone else in the room was distracting you from the commercial, or maybe the ringing of a cell phone had you distracted. You might have been in a bad mood or under the weather, which made the commercial less appealing to you.

But what if you were in a good mood, completely focused, and watched the entire commercial? There are still possible barriers. The actors in the commercial could be annoying, the storyline of the commercial might be odd, or there might be too much music in the background. The product's price, shape, or even its color could be a turn-off.

Have you ever seen a commercial, which after a while, you completely forgot about the product? Often, the commercial creators try to be unique or so funny that they simply forget to sell the product to the consumer, and we just remember the laugh. In other words, there are several reasons why a television commercial's message is not completely received. Even the best marketing firms understand that the consumer only receives 70% to 90% of the message.

So, how is Dr. Woal's theory on advertising messaging applicable to service organizations? It's exactly the same. Oftentimes, the message sent from key leadership is not received by the employees. Inherently, this has a tremendous impact on the team and the customer experience. Lack of communication breeds doubt and confusion. It can make employers question their duty, obligations, position in the organization, and even their worth. It makes them wonder how the organization is doing in general.

To improve our personal communication, first, we must focus on *nonverbal and verbal language.*

## Types of Language

- Tone
- Body Language
- The Inflection in Our Voice

- Pitch of Voice
- Facial Expression

It's an oldie but a goodie. "It's not what you say, but how you say it!" These five types of languages ring more truth in a message than the actual message. If we're rushed, frustrated, bored, or hunched over while we're talking, this speaks volumes about us and creates a communication barrier to the message we are trying to deliver. It is our responsibility to manage all types of languages (nonverbal and verbal) whenever we are delivering a message.

Nearly 75% of all communication is non-verbal. This is why (in some cases) nonverbal communication is more significant than verbal communication. Both management and frontline should focus on their energy in the workplace, as it influences the message they give.

To improve our organizational communication, we must focus on *the process and the why*.

## Create a Communication Process

The process should be a consistent protocol on how to roll out information organization-wide. Employees should know this process and understand where to find and access the information. There should be a foundation of *over-communicating* the message. If the process is broad enough, no employee should feel as if they didn't get the message. The communication process should include but not be limited to:

- Email
- Employee intranet
- Staff meetings
- Newsletters
- Video messaging
- Text messaging
- Social media

Years ago, I had a manager who had a very ineffective communication process. He would literally walk down the hallways, yelling the information: *Meeting tomorrow, 2 PM!* Or *Team meeting tomorrow at 2 PM!* No follow-up email, nothing on the bulletin board. The only information we got was him yelling it out loud.

What do you think happened? The next day came. It was 2 PM, and half the team was not there.

My manager was furious, saying, "*I told everyone! I walked by every single desk. They should all be here!*"

I thought to myself that must be the worst example of communication I'd ever seen. He never thought that maybe someone on the team wasn't able to hear him or they were busy doing their work at the time he walked by them. What if someone was in the restroom or on break? With any of these possibilities, the employee might not be aware of the meeting. As a leader, it is not our job to simply send information, but it's also our job to make sure it was received.

Depending on the scope of the information, it might be necessary to have an *organization town hall*. For town halls to be effective, leadership must offer more than one session at different times of the day. This will ensure that all team members have the opportunity to attend the session. If necessary, have a virtual town hall so employees can login and ask questions live on video or in the chat field. The challenging side of having a town hall is that it is very time-consuming. The positive side is, this immediately puts the organization on a path to getting on the same page.

Town halls are a great opportunity to:

- Share information in a real-time setting
- Gives clarity to the information
- Allows for immediate feedback and dialog

- Sets the stage for *buy-in* from the employees

In an interview with John Maxwell and the CEO of Delta Airlines Ed Bastian, Ed shares a fantastic story of the 2005 bankruptcy filing of Delta. It was a very difficult time for the organization as employees who stayed on had to take massive pay cuts, including pilots who took a whopping 50% pay cut to keep their jobs. Rather than just sending out an email or having supervisors relay information, Delta's leadership decided to create a town hall setting in Atlanta called *The Velvet Series*. The town halls lasted a day and a half. The meeting was not just an information dump on the employees, but an interactive Q&A session for the employees moderated by the CEO and COO. Delta started with just the flight attendants but eventually progressed through all 50,000 employees. Ed Bastian attributes the future success of Delta to these town hall meetings.

Below are some outcomes that were generated following these meetings.

- Delta implemented an Employee Profit Sharing Plan, which meant 15% of all profit went to the employees. This dividend is paid out every Valentine's Day. Ed Bastian says, "We're a company with a heart!"

- In terms of operations, Delta committed to its employees to improve the problem with canceled flights. Canceled flights were the single biggest complaint from customers and the biggest challenge for gate agents, customer service reps, sales agents, and flight attendants. In 2010, Delta had 5,200 cancelations due to mechanical issues. By 2018, they only had 75.

Ed Bastian said, "It's much easier for our employees to be proud of a product that works."

## Explain the Why

It is very important that the leadership of a company shares not only information but also the reason behind it. Oftentimes, employees have questions pertaining to new information that is rolling out. If those questions are not answered, they can become a communication barrier, as we discussed earlier. Some employees just can't get past the reasoning and are almost paralyzed at that moment. If we explain *the why* it will help them process the information.

I'll never forget the time when I was invited to speak at a Washington D.C. government event. The director informed me that she was getting a lot of pushback and negative comments in the hallways about the upcoming event. The yearly event was called the "*All Hands-on Deck*" meeting. After some quick research, I found out that the prior year, the previous director had held this meeting and laid off a quarter of the staff. He literally handed out severance checks at the meeting. I shared with the director that the employees probably thought the same thing would happen this time. She was shocked. She realized that she was not there last year, so she had no idea about this meeting disaster. She asked me for my suggestion of changing their attitude.

First, I suggested changing the name of the meeting. *All Hands-on Deck* is actually a term from the Navy. During a life or death naval battle, the captain orders all personnel on deck to fight. Using this term for a staff meeting, subconsciously creates a mindset of an ensuing battle or war. She changed the name of the meeting to "*Jumpstart Our Success.*"

Second, I suggested that the senior director should send out a video message apologizing for what happened the previous year and ensure to the team that this would not happen at the new meeting.

Simply put, the leaders needed to acknowledge the pain that the previous meeting caused and address the concerns of the employees.

Finally, explain the why. Why are we having this meeting? It turned out that the purpose of the meeting was just an update on the progress for the fiscal year, awards and recognition, and plans for the rollout of the new service initiative. Explaining *the why* relieved a lot of tension and stress for the employees.

*Being the light* means managing the message and keeping communication a top priority. In doing so, it makes your organization much more productive and keeps your employees happy. The CEB (Corporate Executive Board) report states that companies, where managers are high-performing communicators, benefit from productive strategies, successful change initiatives, and positive employee engagement.

> *"If you don't give employees information...*
> *they'll make something up to fill the void!"*

*-Carla O'Dell*

*"While others search for what they can take, a true King searches for what he can give."*

*-Mufasa, The Lion King*

# Chapter 4
# The Foundation of Leadership

The other day, I was watching the Lion King on Disney+ with my family and heard Mufasa tell Simba, *"While others search for what they can take, a true King searches for what he can give."* Suddenly, I grabbed the remote and paused the movie. My family thought I was crazy, but I had to get a pen and write that down. I even hit rewind just to be certain that I got it right. *What a great reminder*, I thought to myself. To have the mindset of *"searching for what we can give,"* is a perfect quote for a promising leader.

How can you *be the light* in your leadership? It is by using the skill of your positive projection and focusing on your team. Leadership is all about serving others. Ask yourself this question: Why do people follow leaders? The simple answer could be that they have to because it is their job. But are they really following the leader or just going through the motions? People follow leaders because of some distinct qualities.

- ▲ Professionalism
- ▲ Skillset
- ▲ Ability
- ▲ Trust
- ▲ Transparency
- ▲ Recognition of employees

One quality that is often overlooked is belief. What does the leader believe? What drives them, and can they passionately communicate their belief to the team?

## What's Your Buffalo?

Years ago, I had a rare1 opportunity to be a stand-in for a movie called *Toy Soldiers*. Just to be clear, stand-ins are not stunt people. Stand-ins are typically hired because they are the same height, weight, and complexion of an actor in the film. Stand-ins are typically not on camera, but they are used to set the light and camera angles, so the real actors won't have to stand all day for practice settings. The stand-in exits as soon as the director yells, "Actors on set!"

It was a great experience. I was a stand-in for Oscar-winning actor Louis Gossett Jr. I got to see how movies were made and witness all the details that go behind the production. One of the many things I learned was that some employees working on a movie set are part of a union and only work on certain parts of the movie. They travel from one movie set to another, filling in on various roles. This played out in real life when we were having lunch one day, and two new production assistants joined our movie set. They sat right across from me and explained that they were on a movie set in Wyoming and just joined our crew. They couldn't have been any more than 24 years old, and they were complaining about the movie set that they were on.

One of them said it was a total disaster and embarrassing. The other one said that she would not even put it on her resume. I had to ask, "What happened?" They began to explain that it was the worst experience of their lives. They said, "The director" (she actually did use air quotes) had this vision to bring in real-life buffaloes on set. *Buffaloes!* These are 2000-pound animals and were totally out of control. We had one night to get the shot, and it was a disaster. I was so glad to be out of there and just knew that movie would be a flop. I thought to myself, "Oh well, I'm just glad to be here." So, I let them vent and continued with my lunch. I stayed three more months for the remainder of this movie shoot. I made a lot of great friends and have some cherished memories.

Two years later, I was in a movie theater and watching a movie with a few of my friends. Out of nowhere, I see a buffalo. I almost thought I was dreaming. I started pointing at the screen, saying, *Buffalo. Those are buffaloes. I can't believe it. I'm looking at buffaloes!*" My friends told me to calm down, but I knew this had to be the movie those two production assistants were talking about. How many buffalo movies can there be? This had to be it. It dawned on me how terrible those two girls said the movie was.

But this movie was not terrible. It was fantastic. In fact, the buffalo scene was amazing and had a huge impact on the movie. The movie I was watching was called *Dances with Wolves*—the movie gained a lot of fame and recognition winning seven Academy Awards including, Best Picture and Best Director. The director of the movie was Kevin Costner.

Curiosity got the better of me, and I had to research and get some background information on this movie. I found out that the buffalo scene was going to cost the movie studio extra money, but Kevin Costner fought for that scene. He needed to get the funding from the studio to get the buffalo scene in the movie. He believed that the buffaloes were very important to complete the story. He wanted to show how the Native Americans respected and honored the buffalo and needed them for food and clothing. It was a powerful message. As the director, his belief and passion about the buffalo was palpable. It was a source of inspiration for his team and the studio.

This is a great reminder of the power of your beliefs as a leader. A great way to get your team to follow you, is to share with your team. Share your passion, your vision, and your beliefs. My question is: What's your buffalo as a leader? What is the initiative, project, or cultural footprint you want to make with your organization? Your team will follow authentic and passionate principles. Share with your team what drives you, so together you can move the needle forward for the team and the organization.

To get your team to believe in your *buffalo*, you must connect with your team. True leaders are those who know how to nurture a rapport with their team. Rather than expecting their team to build a connection with them. Follow these four principles:

## Be Collaborative and Don't Lead by Assumption

Bad leaders tend to just give direction but never ask questions. Great leaders realize it's more important to bring everyone in on an idea, ask questions, and get their input. Even if you have the *buffalo* idea, get feedback from the team. What's the most productive way to make it happen? Is it by financial means, through bandwidth, or strategy? Your team will feel more ownership of the *buffalo* and accept it as their own if they are involved in the process from the early stages.

## Implement Psychological Safety

This is a theory introduced in the book *The Power of Habit* by Charles Duhigg. This is when the leader sets a foundation at meetings where every employee is free to speak and participate. Psychological safety means there is no retribution or criticism. This allows employees to be open to contribute and give their ideas or just brainstorm to create productive ideas. Great leaders use psychological safety to get the best out of their team.

## Coach Up Your Negative Employees for the Benefit of Your Good Employees

*"Nothing kills the spirit of a good employee faster...than the leader tolerating the attitude and actions of a bad employee!"*

*-Perry Belcher*

It's amazing how often I hear story after story of a leader ignoring their negative employees. I guess the leader is using the *hope and pray* method when not confronting an employee who is having a negative impact on your workplace. Meaning, they *hope and pray* it will get better. But it rarely does on its own and is devastating for your good employees.

Take ownership of your negative employees. Have a one-on-one meeting with them and find out where their negativity is stemming from. Support them and give them a chance to change. But unfortunately, if you can't find common ground, you may need to speak with human resources about the next steps. The Walt Disney Company has a phrase that says, *"Negative employees may have to find their happiness elsewhere!"*

## Great Leaders Can Be Trusted to Get Things Done

Do you know anyone in your organization who you can trust to get things done? I'm sure you do. For whatever reason, they have the ability to make the right phone call, ask the right person, and move the project to the next step to help you or the team. Employees follow leaders because they trust that they will get things done. I never realized how big of a trait this really was.

I left college for one semester, before my senior year, to travel overseas in a USO show. I was the company manager for *Kings Six*, and we traveled to South Korea, Japan, Okinawa, and Hawaii to perform for the military. It is still one of the greatest honors of my life.

As the company manager, I was in charge of payroll, reports, and all logistics for travel. One of my biggest challenges was getting our sound equipment safely from one military base to another military base. I clearly remember the flight from Osaka, Japan to Okinawa. It was only supposed to be a two-hour trip, but a bad storm delayed our flight for up to eight hours. When the storm calmed down, we finally boarded and arrived in Okinawa, but our sound equipment did not arrive with us. I had a pit in my stomach, knowing we had a performance the next night for 1500 Marines. So, I called the commanding officer at Kadena Air Base in Okinawa to inform him that we had arrived, but our sound equipment was still in Japan. He jumped on the phone to Osaka, found our eight cases, and got them to Okinawa on the next flight. By the time everything arrived in Okinawa, it was two am. I arranged to have our escort drive me to the airport in a van to pick up our equipment. But by the time we returned to the base, I had a new problem.

We were performing in the gymnasium, and it was locked for the night. I didn't want to wake up the commanding officer, so I asked the escort if there was a shed or locker, we could store the equipment in for the night. Luckily, he found an available storage shed near the maintenance compound on the other side of the base. We drove over and packed the cases in the shed, and I finally went to bed.

The next morning, I called maintenance, and they agreed to bring our sound equipment over to the gymnasium. The escort and I went to the gymnasium to wait for the equipment and scout out the performance area. About that time, the commanding officer and the executive officer showed up and asked me if I had received the sound equipment. I told them we picked it up from the airport late last night but had nowhere to store it, so we arranged to put it in a storage shed by the maintenance compound; and that we were having it delivered shortly.

The executive officer had an uncertain look on his face, but the commanding officer smiled and said, "If Darryl says the equipment is in the shed, then it's in the shed. He's got it covered." He patted me on the back as he left the gymnasium. That was a proud moment for me as a young leader. I'll be honest, as the events of the late flight and sound equipment were unfolding, I was just trying not to make a mess of things and ruin the USO show. The commanding officer's words empowered me immensely. I realized that I was growing as a leader, and I had the ability to be trusted to get things done.

Leadership is always evolving and constantly changing. Remember, *being the light* in your leadership is an important part of your foundation. It's your core belief and passion as a leader. It's how you collaborate, involve, and coach your team. But the most important part of leadership is how you serve and remove barriers so others can succeed.

*"A leader is like a shepherd. He stays behind the flock, letting the most nimble go out ahead, whereupon the others follow, not realizing that all along that they are being directed from behind."*

*-Nelson Mandela*

> *"As the challenge escalates,
> the need for teamwork elevates."*
>
> **- John Maxwell**

# Chapter 5
# Empowering the Team

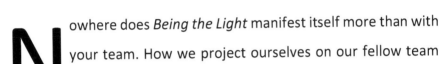

**N**owhere does *Being the Light* manifest itself more than with your team. How we project ourselves on our fellow team members dictates their level of productivity, quality, and customer service.

Once, I was hired to be the keynote speaker at an annual customer service conference for a commercial builder in Sarasota, FL. Prior to the event, I had a great conversation with the Director of H.R. I wanted to be sure that I learned all I could about the organization and what she needed me to incorporate in the presentation. She wanted me to motivate the troops about customer service, talk about managing change, leadership, and, most importantly, include a team-building discussion with activities. I thought that was great!

So, I asked, "Just so I can align my content and team building activity to yours, what has your organization done throughout this year in terms of team building and employee engagement?"

Her response was...silence! Unfortunately, this is all too common. Although she is a great leader, she was very well aware that, as an organization, they had not taken the time to invest and engage with their employees as they should have. Soon, it became her personal mission to change that reality.

To assist, I shared with her my story about the *Best Lawn in the Neighborhood*. Years ago, my wife and I purchased a home in Prince William County, Virginia. It was in a beautiful location and was a prime investment property. If we ever wanted to rent it out, we would have plenty of possible renters. It was 10 minutes from Quantico Marine Corps Base and a 35-minute drive to the Pentagon. Well, that was with no traffic. With traffic, it would take three days.

Anyway, as customary, my wife and I would walk the neighborhood every sunset. We couldn't help but notice one house down the street that had the most beautiful yard. It looked like something off of the PGA tour. I literally thought one could chip and putt off his lawn. It was green, lush, and very healthy. It was by far the best lawn in the neighborhood. I was always in awe of the quality of this lawn. I thought to myself, "How did he get his lawn to look like that? Why did my lawn look average at best?"

Finally, on one of our sunset walks, that homeowner was outside, so I approached and asked him about his lawn. He was more than happy to coach me up on lawn maintenance. We discussed everything from types of lawnmowers, grass, seeds, bushes, plants, watering, and even the benefits and pitfalls of the sun. But it was his mentality on creating a healthy lawn that stood out to me.

He said, "Anyone who is thinking about having a great lawn always talks about what they're going to pull out. And obviously, they're referring to weeds." As I nodded, he continued, "Yes, you should manage the weeds in your lawn. But what makes a beautiful, healthy lawn isn't so much what you're pulling out; it's what you're putting in." That statement really resonated with me. He said, "Here's the secret. What you put into your lawn to make it healthy and strong is fertilizer, which is rich with nitrogen."

I didn't know that. It turns out that nitrogen not only kills your weeds, but it also nourishes the soil and the existing grass in your lawn. So, when you go to your local Home Depot or Lowe's, look for a fertilizer that is rich in nitrogen. I took his advice and transformed my lawn in a few short months to the *Best Lawn in the Neighborhood*.

I got an award and finally dethroned the king. He didn't mind. It was all in fun trying to beat each other. I have to say; I'm still proud of that.

His words had a big impact on me. "It's not so much what you're pulling out; it's what you're putting in." I think that is the perfect correlation to empowering and building a great team. It is very easy to ask how we can pull out that aggravating employee or get rid of that difficult personality. But the bigger question should be, what are we putting into our team? What are we doing to pour empowerment and engagement into our team? Much like healthy grass, it's what you put in the lawn that makes it so healthy.

Empowering the team means we are taking a group of individually contributing employees and transforming their mindset into cohesive team contributors. The first step in this process is understanding that we cannot buy our team. Meaning, we cannot ignore their need for engagement and development throughout the entire year and then decide to do a quick Friday night team-building bowling night. Even though it pains me to say, you can't just hire a keynote speaker to build the team in 60 minutes. It just doesn't work that way. Don't get me wrong; team outings are very important and can assist in connecting with the team members. But the team outings cannot be the team building. Team building actually happens day in and day out, in the workplace.

## Benefits of Empowering Your Employees:

### An Engaged Staff

When you have healthy engagement in your workplace, employees feel it, and they redirect that positivity to their clients and colleagues. Perhaps, the ideal approach to improve engagement is to give workers a say in how the company should move forward. At the point when they become a part of the solution, they feel more connected and remain emotionally involved.

### Adapting to Change

Some companies get stuck and become stagnant by not considering their employees' needs. Investing in technology that can make it easier and accessible for employees to complete their tasks is always a good idea for engagement. For this, you need input from your working staff. When you listen and communicate with your employees, the entire team can adapt to the changes at work, and everyone can stay in the loop. Frequently asking your employees for thoughts on innovation and systems that could improve the efficiency of your business, is an incredible method to keep your business at the forefront of productivity.

## Attracting New Talent

When you form an engaged workforce, you will instantly pull in new employees who will flourish in this healthy and cooperative work environment. Professionals who are self-sufficient and step up to the plate will start to pay heed to your organization. After some time, your entire workplace culture will transform for the better.

## Feeling Appreciated

To draw in your staff, you need to become more acquainted with them on a personal level. This will improve your work relationship and make it easier to understand each other's demands. Know your team's likes and dislikes, and most importantly, recognize them. This doesn't have to be monetary. Start by saying, "Thank you." Or "I appreciate your work." Recognizing your employees goes a long way to making them feel appreciated.

# Empowering Your Team

## Professional & Personal Development Opportunities

This can range from access to general online learning to professional certification training. Employees want to feel as if they can grow not only in the role, but also in education.

When I was a young emerging leader, I remember my director providing a professional development assessment for the team. I learned so much from that assessment. For example, I've never truly enjoyed brainstorming sessions. It always felt like we would brainstorm, just for the sake of brainstorming. In other words, we wouldn't do anything afterward. I did not like that. The assessment results taught me that my trait is an *Activator*, which means I want to get stuff done. Hence, I am not very productive when I'm just brainstorming for nothing. I don't mind brainstorming, as long as we agree to pick one of the ideas and do it afterward. The assessment made me understand myself and how I can implement what I learned.

## Stretch Goals

These are extended goals that put an employee in charge of a real and specific assignment with accountabilities that exceed the expectations of their current role. This allows employees to develop the skillset and abilities that align with an advanced position.

The stretch assignment that had the biggest impact on my life was during my senior year in college when I interned for an HR director. Part of my job was to sit in with the director as she led group job interviews. I listened to all her questions and learned how she narrowed down the field for follow-up interviews. She gave me a stretch goal, challenging me to get out of my comfort zone and run my own set of interviews without her. It was a big learning experience, and I quickly realized that the hiring manager has so much to consider when bringing on a new employee. To this day, I use some of the strategies that I was taught.

## Involvement Currency

This is a mental and emotional *perceived* engagement currency that is earned and given from the employee to the leader. When the leader spends time with their team and assists in the successes and challenges throughout the day, a perceived and inherent currency is built up with the leader.

## The Power of Involvement Currency

I led an employee focus group at a large call center in Las Vegas, Nevada. This company booked vacation packages to Las Vegas and helicopter flights to the Grand Canyon. The client had a large account with the British travel firm Thomas Cook, so the phones were constantly ringing. In the call center, there were two managers, Vanessa and Cathy. After some initial research, I found out that all of the call center reps loved Vanessa and did not like Cathy.

At first, I thought this had to be a coincidence. Was it possible Vanessa was just nicer? Maybe Cathy managed with more discipline and held the team more accountable. Not at all. After facilitating the focus group and reviewing all the comments, it was quite clear. There was one reason why the reps loved Vanessa and did not like Cathy. Vanessa got involved, and Cathy didn't. That was it! The employees shared with me that they were critiqued, judged, and compensated on *speed to* and *time on* the phone. When they were overwhelmed with calls, Cathy sat in her office and just let the call center reps drown in overwhelming phone calls. This caused tremendous resentment because the team felt as if she did it on purpose. Obviously, there were times she was too busy and couldn't help, but there were definitely other times when she could help out...but just didn't.

However, when Vanessa was available, she would get on the phone and assist the team. That's the power of Involvement Currency. She was building up the currency with her team by being in the trenches, empowering her team, and helping them succeed. She thought of herself as part of the team, whereas Cathy thought of herself as merely managing the team.

**Question**: *Which manager do you think was the true team builder?*

After 11 months of working with Vanessa, if she decided to have a team outing, it would only elevate and enhance the team she had already built. However, if after 11 months, Cathy decided to have a team outing, it would come across staged and not very genuine. She hadn't built up any currency with her team.

## Identify Your S.T.s

The final criteria for empowering your team is to know your team. The traits, characteristics, and personalities can be understood by ST's. Who are the *ST's* on your Team?

1. Stinger: The Stinger is an inherently negative employee. They typically see the glass as half empty and are usually the last ones to *buy-in* to any project or initiative. But don't give up on the stinger. Although they can be difficult, if you turn them around, it will gain tremendous points from your team.

2. **Stronger:** The Stronger is a type-A personality that is focused solely on work. They typically do not want to join in on the company picnic. They have a difficult time working with someone who is not working hard. Although I would like to see Stronger a little friendlier in the workplace, their productivity is intense, and they get the job done.
3. **Stander:** Just like it sounds, the Stander loves to stand around and socialize. They are the life of the party and don't miss the company picnic. Although they focus a bit too much on personal connection and are somewhat of an *over talker*, they are positive and upbeat employees.
4. **Stabilizer:** Stabilizers are the steady hand of your team. They have the ability to navigate through many situations while keeping the team top of mind. They have big shoulders and are trusted by the leadership. They know the pulse of the project and the team.

You may have all four personality traits on your team. Sometimes, you have an employee with more than one of the traits. Regardless, to empower your team, you need to understand your team. It seems reasonable to try and coerce everyone to move into the stabilizer category, but that is not realistic. Just as I learned from my professional development assessment, some of your teams' traits are part of their DNA. Unfortunately, *Stingers* are negatively impacting your team, so they need your attention and direction. We'll get more into managing conflict in the next chapter, but for now, you need to understand the interpersonal dynamics of your team. Former Super Bowl-winning coach of the Dallas Cowboys, Jimmy Johnson, said, *"I treat all my players fairly...but I don't treat them the same."* Good advice for empowering your team. They all need something a little different.

Leaders must use the perfect mix of motivation, recognition, accountability, and counseling to guide their employees. The ultimate goal is to let your team members grow and help them develop into the best versions of themselves.

*"Peace is not the absence of conflict,
but the ability to cope with it."*

*-Mahatma Gandhi*

## Chapter 6
## Lean into Conflict

As a corporate trainer, one of the most frequent questions I receive is: How can I *be the light* at work, when there is conflict lingering in the workplace? This is an understandable question because the very nature of conflict seems completely the opposite of *being the light* or showing a positive projection.

My answer remains the same. *Being the light* is the necessary component of conflict resolution. Why? Because *being the light* shapes your mindset. It acknowledges that the goal in conflict isn't to win the fight. The goal is first to understand...that it is not a fight at all.

*"Conflict is inevitable, but combat is optional."*

*-Max Lucado*

Unfortunately, conflict can be a regular occurrence in the workplace and can hinder the working environment for a just a couple of employees or sometimes the entire organization.

The working environment can turn sour when the people in charge allow conflict to grow as opposed to dealing with it and working it out. Often, leaders prefer to stay away from the conflict letting employees deal with it themselves. What they don't understand is that by maintaining a strategic distance from the conflict, they are mistakenly creating internal problems among the employees. Leaders should neutralize or limit conflict and not allow it to develop and spin out of control.

Just like the root cause of many life problems, poor communication plays the biggest part in workplace conflicts. Mistaken assumptions, closed-mindedness, and behaving passive-aggressively can all add up to creating an unhealthy working environment because of unresolved conflicts.

Here are the two basic types of conflict:

- **High-Yielding Conflict**: Conflict that looks to support mutually agreed-upon solutions. High-yielding conflict produces a high return for positive outcomes. Employees seek understanding and value the solution over themselves.

➤ **Low-Yielding Conflict**: Conflict that looks to *win* at all costs. Low-yielding conflict produces a low return for positive outcomes. Employees seek quick conclusions and value themselves over the solution.

It's important to realize that high-yielding conflict can benefit the organization and the team. Instead of trying to sweep everything under the rug to reach a quick solution, focus on understanding the conflict, which opens the door for an agreement.

Regardless, conflict remains challenging because within high-yielding and low-yielding conflict, it breaks down into two distinct areas: customer and employee conflict. Let's look at both.

## Customer Conflict: *Major McBryant*

During the summer between my freshman and sophomore year in college, I worked at Herman's sporting goods. I manned the fitness shoe department and took the job very seriously. Whenever it was slow, I would try on the shoes, so that I would have first-hand knowledge of the style, fit, and quality of the shoe. I was known as the most knowledgeable salesperson in the store when it came to our shoes. If I saw you, I could guess your shoe size within half an inch of your shoe size. My *"shoe size guessing ego"* was through the roof!

One afternoon, a rough and somewhat loud military man came into the store. He was the kind of guy who you could hear before you could see him. I was in the back area, stocking shoes, when I heard him yell, "Is anyone working here?"

I quickly realized he must be standing in the shoe department, so I went onto the sales floor. There I met Major McBryant. Because I was a military kid myself, I understood ranks and could recognize the insignias on his uniform. He was wearing his green fatigues, I clearly saw the gold clusters on his shoulders, and it said McBryant on his jacket.

In a gruff and raspy voice, he said to me, "I want the best running shoe you've got!"

I paused because I knew there was no such thing. It really all depended on your purpose for the shoe. I asked, "Major McBryant, we have many different types of shoes. Are you running on asphalt, cross country, or is this for PT at the base?"

He cut me off and said, "I want the best running shoe you've got!" It was starting to get a little embarrassing, and I just wanted to end this. So, I responded politely, "I understand, is there a certain price point you want to stay within?"

He yelled even louder, "Look, I want the best running shoe you've got, size 10!"

First of all, I knew he was a size 10, but I didn't get a chance to impress him with my *"Jedi shoe guessing skills!"* Second, at this point, my manager was staring at me from across the store, expecting me to handle this customer. So, I quickly went in the back and grabbed the Nike Odyssey. The Nike Odyssey was our flagship shoe and cost $105. At that time, other than the Nike Air Jordan, it was the most expensive shoe that we had. I walked onto the sales floor with the box and said, "Major McBryant, this is the Nike odyssey, it's $105," and handed it to him.

He paused, stared at the shoe, and said, "Give me the second-best running shoe you've got!"

Now, we kind of started laughing. This tough and rough guy only talked this way because he thought this was the way to be assertive. Although he was a difficult customer, I learned a very important lesson about customer conflict: *Don't take it personally!* He turned out to be harmless. By the way, he ended up leaving the store with a pair of ASICS Gels for $39.

*Don't take it personally!* This is not always the easiest phrase to hear. Let's face it; when you're in the middle of a customer conflict, it feels personal. But that statement is still true, try not to take it personally. I believe every customer and employee has their own truth based on their past experiences. Sometimes, these experiences were negative, and they resurface in the current situation with you. So, there are times that the inner conflict surfacing with another person isn't about you. The situation simply reminds them of past negative experiences and creates *Red Flags*!

## Employee Conflict: *The Curling Iron*

My wife, Jennifer, is a dance teacher and takes her craft very seriously. Not only does she create her own curriculum and dance choreography, but she also often goes to dance conferences for additional education and training. Periodically, she travels to New York to take a master class from one of her many dancer friends on Broadway. Three months after we were married, Jennifer flew to New York with her girlfriend Lisa to take a master class from her good friend on Broadway.

I stayed home. This was before we had children, so I found myself alone in the house with just the dog for the entire weekend. It was my first time alone since Jennifer, and I had started dating two years earlier. I stayed very busy, watching TV, eating, sleeping, and watching more TV. It was exhausting!

Jennifer returned late Sunday afternoon, quickly unpacked, and we caught up on her travels.

Later that evening, I was on the sofa watching the football game when I noticed her in my peripheral vision. She was standing there, glaring at me and holding a curling iron. She said to me, "What's this?" I replied, "I don't know... a curling iron?" I returned to my game. She said, "I know what it is, whose is it?" I said, "I don't know... yours?" Again, I returned to my game.

You must understand I had only been married for three months, so I was not the brightest when it came to husband and wife issues. Looking back on it, I really should have recognized the problem much sooner.

My wife was still standing there and said, "It's not mine!" She sounded very agitated. Now it dawned on me what she was thinking. She thought that when she traveled to New York, and while she was gone, I had another woman over, and that woman left her curling iron in our house.

Being the comedian that I am, I said, "Babe, Halle Berry was here, but she didn't even bring a curling iron!" I have to admit in my head that it was hilarious. But my wife did not find that funny at all. She knew Halle Berry was my celebrity Hollywood crush, but at that point, there was nothing I could do to make her laugh.

I realized I was in big trouble. I could not explain where that curling iron came from. The more I talked, the guiltier I looked. Our house was a resale, so someone else owned the house before us. I actually said, "Is it possible that the curling iron was already here from before we bought the house? Maybe we just never noticed it?" That sounded ridiculous. I was just grasping at straws, trying to explain the existence of this mysterious curling iron.

At this point, my wife was very upset and distanced herself from me. Our first marital conflict had begun, and it was not looking good. The only one that believed me was the dog, but then again…he was a dog.

A few days went by, and my wife called me at work, sounding very enthusiastic. "Hello, sweetheart," she said with the sweetest voice. I was immediately confused. She continued, "I think I know where the curling iron came from."

This got my attention. I said, "I'm all ears."

"I got a phone call from Lisa today. She asked if I accidentally grabbed her curling iron in New York. It hit me like a rock that I did. On our last day in New York, I must have accidentally grabbed her curling iron, packed it in my suitcase, and brought it back to our house. Isn't that crazy?" She said with awe.

I was blown away. "Yeah, real crazy..." I mumbled. "Can I get off the sofa and come back to the bedroom now?"

We have since laughed about that story many times. All was forgiven because I was understood. When Jennifer and I were dating, long before we married, she told me a story of her old boyfriend cheating on her and breaking her heart. The story was painful because she could sense it. Red flags went off about her old boyfriend, but she convinced herself, along with his brainwashing and manipulation, that it was not true. It turned out, it was true, and it took her a long time to get past it. So even though we have a faithful and loving marriage, the second she sensed the red flag, it took her right back to that emotional and hurtful place.

The learning point is, red flags are alive and well with all our employees too. One of the major reasons for conflict in the workplace, is that an employee experiences a red flag. If they had conflict in their previous occupations, the memory might have been burnt into their history. Much like my wife with the curling iron, it is a painful memory that resurfaces because of a recent situation. It really isn't about you, but every employee has a *curling iron red flag* story. New bosses, initiatives, changes in structure, changes in pay, or changing offices can trigger a red flag. It's a truly emotional experience that resembles what they are going through now. The *fight or flight* mentality kicks in, and now you're in the middle of a low-yielding conflict. It's our job as leaders to navigate through the red flags and create a peaceful solution.

I believe, as leaders, we should *Lean into Conflict*. Most try to touch on it briefly or even avoid it altogether. How you manage conflict speaks volumes of you as a leader.

Here are a few best practices.

- **Understand that it matters**: Whether you think it is important or not, always remember it is their story. Honor their struggle. What they have been through in the past matters, and we should give grace and validity to their feelings.

- **De-escalate**: Do you want to make a point or make a difference? If the goal is to be the light, then approach the situation with a mindset of defusing the intensity and look for understanding and solutions.

- **Clarify perceptions**: How many times have you said something to someone, and they misinterpreted your meaning? It could have been what you said or how you said it, but either way, now there is tension. It's our job to communicate clearly and clarify perceptions. Sometimes, the conflict starts because of a simple misunderstanding.

*"The passions are the same in every conflict, large or small."*

*-Mason Cooley*

*"You never know how strong you are until being strong is the only choice you have."*

*-Bob Marley*

# Chapter 7
# The Character of Resilience

**The definition of resilience: n. the ability to bounce back.**

Resilience is the capacity of an individual to stand firm against hardships, keep their balance, have a sense of control, and push ahead in a positive way. Some people navigate this easier and can adapt to unpleasant circumstances compared to others, mostly because of having resilience. These individuals flourish while others around them feel the pressure. Fortunately, being resilient is not unattainable and not something that an individual is born without.

Anyone can learn how to be resilient through practice. A resilient work culture can also be built to support its employees. There are numerous negative working environments that can be difficult such as excessive workload, lack of autonomy, lack of support or teamwork, and constant organizational restructuring that can cause stress for employees. In your work life, you might have encountered a point when you were knocked down, but you got back up. I think it is straightforward to focus or analyze our successes but, *being the light* in the midst of our failure is also an incredible trait. Let's face it; we are going to fail at one point in our lives. We never want to say it or believe it, but failure is a part of life. You may have failed projects, failed businesses, and failed relationships, but this does not mean you are a failure. It does not mean you have to quit. It simply means adversity has arrived, and your level of resilience will be tested.

Long before our first personal failure, we probably have witnessed someone else's failure. It could have been a manager, a coach, or even a parent. What do you remember about how they handled failure? In some cases, we witness an emotional meltdown. There might have been yelling and screaming, and other times we may have noticed a passive-aggressive behavior. Either way, this is our first lesson on how to handle failure. We learn those negative traits must be the only way to handle failure. However, through a certain amount of self-reflection and some introspective practices, you can unlearn this negative response to your failure.

Hopefully, you have also witnessed a positive failure. These people seem to have more control and be less outwardly emotional. It certainly doesn't mean that the issue isn't important to them. I would argue they are just better at navigating failure and have a true character of resilience.

Personal resilience can be learned and improved by focusing on a variety of practices that decrease being vulnerable and susceptible to stress caused by failure. It can likewise assist you in developing and sustaining certain skills for decreasing the effect that difficulty in the work environment has on you.

To have the character of resilience means you understand that failure is sometimes part of the process. Obviously, you do not want to fail, but if you do, your mindset should not be if you can bounce back, but when.

## The Four Pillars of Resilience

### Overcome Self-Doubt

Overcoming self-doubt is the first step to building resilience because it is the most important. There is no way around it. Failing can be a gut punch to your soul. We are identified by our careers, roles, and projects, so when they fall short, it feels like we ourselves are failures.

*How do you overcome self-doubt?* For that, you have to understand the power of conditioning.

My favorite animal is the elephant. I love its grace, power, and desire to be within the family herd. I got a chance to visit the elephant sanctuary in Chiang Mai, Thailand. I was surprised to see that many of the elephants were walking around the grounds, without any restraints. You could buy a bushel of bananas or sugar cane for one dollar and feed the elephants. It was amazing. Later in the afternoon, I got to ride on an elephant in the jungles of Chiang Mai. I sat in a mounted wooden chair on the elephant's back while my guide, Hamm, was sitting on his neck.

During our trek through the bushes and trees, I asked Hamm all I could think about elephants. I wanted to know how these elephants were so calm and walking around freely. I've seen plenty of TV news footage of elephants being very aggressive, knocking over cars, and destroying property. I shared with Hamm that in America, other than a circus, we typically have elephants in zoos. He explained to me that the elephants in this sanctuary are conditioned.

I said, "What do you mean?"

He pointed to a baby elephant and said, "Do you notice the rope around the baby elephant's neck?

I took a look and said, "Yes."

He continued, "It's attached to a stake in the ground. It's part of our training process. For many months to come, that baby elephant will tug and pull trying to get away. Eventually, he will realize that he cannot. So, by the time he is a full-grown elephant, about 8,000 pounds, all I have to do is put this rope around his neck, and he thinks he can't move anywhere. He thinks I am in control. But in reality, he is still in control, but he's just conditioned."

This got me thinking about who else acts like the elephant. Humans do. Self-doubt in humans is a type of conditioning. It's a negative inner belief that is probably resurfacing from a long time ago. What do you believe about yourself? What do you believe about yourself as a leader? The answers to these questions came years ago. Much like the baby elephant, you'll tug and pull, but after a while, you'll believe in less than what you can be. You'll give in to the lie about yourself. That is why you have to break your conditioning through new learning.

In behavioral psychology, conditioning is a very powerful theory that states, "An object or event can be modified by learning." This is great news because psychology tells us, we can modify our thoughts and actions, but it takes learning. When self-doubt creeps into our conscience, we have two options:

## Action or Avoidance

For most people, it is easy to pick avoidance. Our worry, concern, and fear keep us paralyzed with the mindset of "It can't be done." Once you've entered that state, it's difficult to bounce back because you believe it's not possible, so you can't bounce back.

The other option is *action*. It is a powerful step because it is the foundation of resilience. Even though you may not know exactly what to do or how to correct the problem, you still choose to act. The action could be a brainstorming meeting with your team or setting an individual meeting with a trustworthy coach or mentor. It's a choice. You choose to step forward, stay positive, and believe in yourself. Many people don't realize that doubting yourself is actually a choice. Think about it: nothing has happened to you other than your project failing. No official court order or physical limitation is mandating that you have to doubt yourself. You are simply letting your mind choose to doubt.

To clarify, I'm not saying you should never experience fear, concern, or worry. These feelings are real, and no one should pretend these negative emotions don't exist. I'm saying you can't let them cripple your progress. Most importantly, you can't let the doubt take over the dialog in your head.

Have you ever been caught talking to yourself? I don't mean low mumbling noises. I mean full-fledged sentences. Sometimes, I have a clear, articulate, and loud conversation with myself. Almost every time my wife walks into the room and says, "Who are you talking to?" I say, "Myself," and we start laughing. But it's a great reminder that no one talks to you, more than you.

In those moments, when doubt is setting in, ask yourself these questions.

- Why am I choosing doubt?
- How would doubting myself serve my team or me?
- What would the consequences be if I didn't take action?

Overcoming self-doubt does not mean you have all the answers. It just means you're choosing to stay positive, persistent, and vocal. Tell yourself, "Doubt shall not win today!"

## Admit Failure

Be humble and self-aware enough to admit to yourself and your team that you failed. Have you ever been around someone who did not admit when they were wrong? Isn't it frustrating? They want to move on but never acknowledge what happened. It is extremely important that we admit to our team that we, our idea, the projections, whatever failed.

Here is an important distinction about admitting failure. You do not have to make a dramatic self-pity speech or play the martyr. You don't even have to use the word *failure*. Let's say you're the manager of a sales team. You can simply say, "Team, I apologize. We didn't hit our sales target last quarter. I underestimated the slow holiday months. I own that. I'll look for ways to exceed our sales goals next quarter." That's it. Now your team knows you're taking responsibility and so they would be much more willing to forgive and move on. Also, you have given yourself permission to move on. There is nothing lingering, so go to the next step.

But what if it wasn't you? What if your holiday projections were spot-on and your team simply didn't hit their numbers? Remember what we discussed in Chapter 5. As a manager, you are part of the team. "Team, I apologize. We didn't hit our sales target last quarter.

I'll look for ways to help us exceed our sales goals next quarter." Again, that's it. Be genuine and authentic. Now move on.

> "Character is built out of your mistakes. If you went back and re-did all your bad decisions, you wouldn't have the character you have today."
>
> -**Legendary UCLA Basketball Coach John Wooden**

## What Did You Learn?

Asking this is a great trait of a leader. Now that you've admitted failure, it's time to analyze what happened and what you learned. This could be extremely valuable information for projects moving forward.

Milton Hershey admitted failure three times, with three separate candy companies prior to launching Hershey. He learned that selling chocolates individually, or one at a time, was bound to fail. He needed to sell in bulk. So, he launched the Lancaster Caramel Company. His previous failure was now the beginning of his success. He learned how to make sales to the masses. So, he sold the Lancaster Caramel Company to start his milk chocolate company *Hershey's*. The first Hershey bar hit stores in 1900. They were so popular that it allowed Milton to build his own company town of Hershey, Pennsylvania.

I personally love this story because it shows if we learn from our mistakes, we can rise above the challenge. I also love it because in my house we love Hershey bars. When I think about it, there are so many different types of chocolate bars available. But nothing beats the original Hershey bar. It's a good thing for my family that Milton Hershey learned from his failure, or else my wife and I wouldn't have Hershey bars to hide in the back of the refrigerator.

## Reset Your Objectives

You're ready to bounce back. You're positive and up for the challenge. This is a great opportunity to adjust the project moving forward. Re-assess the budget, scope, and duration. But also, be sure to reset the objectives from the lens of Strategy and Tactics.

In the book, *Managing Transitions* by Bill Bridges, there is a simple model called the 4 Ps. The 4 Ps is a great framework to manage Strategy and Tactics.

## The 4 Ps Strategy

- Purpose: *What's our goal for being here as an organization? Who do we serve?*
- Picture: *What does the picture of our future looks like when we are fulfilling our purpose? What are we doing day in and day out better than anyone else?*

## Tactics

- ▲ Plan: *What's the plan that we've created, and we're following through on that helps us create the picture that fulfills the purpose?*
- ▲ Part: *What is your part to play? How do you fit into the plan that helps create the picture that fulfills the purpose?*

This framework is a great way to reset and look at your overall objectives. Being resilient does not always mean jumping back in the saddle and doing the same thing as before. Sometimes, it means re-assessing and taking an over-arching view. Using the 4Ps gives you the lens of a larger perspective.

There is one final ingredient of resilience. It's called *grit*. When trying to bounce back, it's very important to use strategy and best practices because you don't want to lead blindly. But, let's face it, at some point you'll need to roll up your sleeves and push through it. You've done it before. Think back on a time when the odds were stacked against you, and you pushed through. Yes, it may not have been the exact same situation, but you've proven that you already have grit in you. Do it again. How can you Be the Light in difficult times? By showing the character of your resilience: Resolve, Character, and Courage.

BE THE LIGHT!

> *"Differences can be the sources of creativity, or they can serve to divide."*
>
> *-Craig Runde*

## Chapter 8
## Our Differences Make the Difference

Have you ever had a co-worker who loved to tell jokes? I had one. Meet my former co-worker, Rob MacIntire. He was the kind of guy who wished in his dream life that he would be a stand-up comedian. The only problem was that he wasn't that funny. He told corny Dad jokes almost every day. There were times I would try to hide when I saw him coming down the hallway. So, we dealt with the MC (Master of Corny) as best we could. But honestly, at least Rob was harmless. What happens when we have personalities in the workplace that are not harmless?

Sometimes, navigating different types of people and personalities in the workplace can be difficult. Certain employees don't see things the way you do or work through a project the way you do. It can be annoying because it's different and adjusting to it can also be difficult.

Typically, we don't like things that are different. We want things nice and easy, just the way we do things. However, to *be the light* means you have to embrace differences and understand the power in your diversity.

> *"Diversity is the art of thinking independently, together."*
>
> **-*Malcolm Forbes***

Every person is unique. Everyone comes into a workplace with a unique set of life experiences, beliefs, and identities. According to resources.workable.com, here are some of the various types of diversity observed in the workplace today:

- Cultural Diversity
- Financial Diversity
- Racial and Ethnic Diversity
- Religious Diversity
- Age Diversity
- Sex and Gender Diversity
- Sexual Orientation
- Disability

The different categories of diversity are equally important. Depending on your corporate makeup, one might be more prevalent than the other. In my career, surprisingly, I've experienced age diversity the most.

Because of our age, we have certain biases, attitudes, and preferences built in our generation.

**The Greatest Generation** (born 1922-1945) are extremely hard workers, very patriotic, and feels a personal responsibility for supporting the nation in a time of crisis. They respect authority based on the title alone; however, the Greatest are set in their ways and privately can be somewhat stubborn.

**Baby Boomers** (born 1946-1964) are also extremely hard workers. They *Live to Work*. Boomers have a difficult time working next to someone who is not working hard. This generation has the challenge of juggling elderly parents and high school or college-aged children. This is the first generation to question authority.

**Generation X** (born 1965-1980) Xers have more of a *Work to Live* mentality. Created PTO (paid time off), Xers had a minor introduction to the technology, with computers, ATMs, and cable news. They are called the *latch key kids* because many of their moms went back to work, leaving them with a key under the mat to get inside of the house. This gave Xers a sense of independence that they have brought into the workplace.

**Millennials** (born 1981-2002) are born into technology. They have always known computers and the internet. Millennials have an entrepreneurial spirit. In the workplace, they want to be developed and coached. They don't want a job. They want a life. Sometimes, millennials are looked upon as though they are entitled. I often say it's not their fault. If I was born into Apple, Microsoft, and Starbucks, I might be a little entitled too. Millennials really do want things better, faster, stronger, and quicker. Soon to be the largest generation in the workplace, millennials want to work with less authority but more inclusion.

**Gen Z:** Take everything from Millennials and add Uber, Grub Hub, Airbnb, and Streaming Services, you have Gen Z.

Never underestimate the inherent traits or characteristics that come from your generation. It shapes our point of view and mindset. It's not right or wrong; it's simply different.

As leaders, the first step in building on the positivity from our differences is through the awareness of our differences. For example, have you ever heard a leader say, "I don't see color on my team?" Or "I'm color blind." I understand that the leader is trying to imply that they treat everyone the -same, and there is no prejudice in their actions. But in reality, leaders **should** see color. They should see gender, age, disability, and all the wonderful differences we embody. John Maxwell says, *"Diversity fills in the perspective, knowledge and experience gap."*

Great leaders understand that diversity is nothing to be concerned or threatened by. They know the differences in their team can only elevate their projects.

- Creativity: Diverse teams bring different ideas and perspectives to a project. Because of the different backgrounds, creativity flourishes, and unique variations can be implemented.

- Productivity: Diverse teams bring high quality and effectiveness to a project. They can see a project from different points of view and provide the leader with distinct options.

So, rather than a leader saying, "I don't see color on my team!" The leader should say, "I lead a wonderfully diverse team." Or "The diversity on my team is one of our strongest attributes." But diversity alone will not make a positive difference. You need inclusion.

Diversity is an awareness by the leader. Inclusion is a choice by the leader.

Inclusion, as defined by SHRM (Society for Human Resources Management), is *"The achievement of a work environment, in which all individuals are treated fairly and respectfully, have equal access to opportunities and resources, and can contribute fully to the organization's success."*

According to Inclusion Expert and Co-Founder of Mix Diversity Hayley Barnard, the four traits of the inclusive leader are **F.A.S.T.**

1. **Fair:** Inclusive leaders treat people fairly and equally.
2. **Action:** Inclusive leaders take action, demanding participation from everyone on the team.
3. **Self-aware:** Inclusive leaders understand they have biases, and they might have organizational blind spots. They ask themselves, "What's it like from your point of view?"
4. **Trust Builder:** Inclusive leaders trust their team members and are committed to 'we' before 'me.' Fostering trust will enable team members to contribute their unique perspectives.

To *Be the Light* as a leader, you should be cognizant of differences. You understand that the world is diverse, so it only makes sense that the team and the organization are a representation of what we see. These leaders are ready and willing to take the action of inclusion. But does a diverse team really make a difference? It is completely understandable when some leaders ask the question, "can you prove it?" To put it this way, does being more diverse and inclusive actually affect the bottom line, or is this all simply anecdotal information?

Well, I'm glad you asked! In 2017, the report *Delivering through Diversity* from McKinsey & Company stated that companies have a greater likelihood of making higher profits, when their senior management has a more diverse representation. The latest data showed an increase of 21%.

In 2017, the Boston Consulting Group (BCG) established thorough research that a 19% increase in revenue is observed by including diversity. In the Insights Newsletter BCG Partner, Rocio Lorenzo explained how teams establish themselves on the basis of diverse leadership and then thrive. Through the BCG study, they found that financial performance shows a better innovation when the diversity of their leadership team is increased. The sample study took 1700 various companies under consideration, spanning across eight different countries. All of these were from different industrial backgrounds and varying strengths and sizes.

Finally, as we discussed earlier, Millennials are quickly becoming the largest generation in the workplace. 75% of the workforce worldwide is expected to be comprised of millennials by the year 2025. Major leadership roles and decision-makers will be predominantly millennials. This generation has by far the most inclusive of mindsets of all the previous generations. They support diversity and inclusion policies and practices. In their opinion, an ideal workplace is one that uplifts its employees by giving every opinion a chance to be voiced on a suitable platform.

- The 2016 Deloitte Millennial Survey indicates that diversity and inclusion are some of the most sought-for traits when considering an employer by 47% of millennials.

- The 2018 Deloitte Millennial Survey revealed that when organizations have a more inclusive culture, 74% of the millennials consider label them as innovative.

It seems apparent that practicing diversity and inclusion will improve your bottom line.

In 2010, I did some consulting work for a midsize DC government contractor. They were located just outside the Beltway. Although they usually obtained smaller accounts, they were very competitive in bidding on high-level government contracts. In the most recent months, they found themselves losing out to Lockheed Martin, Raytheon, and Bae Systems for larger and more lucrative contracts.

The company culture was decent, but there was nothing to brag about. The director was a 60-year-old white male and a former major in the army. He was definitely not prejudiced and was aware of diversity. I think his only area of growth opportunity was that he was not very inclusive. During any of the decision-making meetings, he had the same five assistant directors in the room. They were all white men, former military, and about his age.

I'm not at all saying that I should've been in the room. I'm saying Esmeralda should've been in the room. Esmeralda Rodriguez, who we called Ezzie, was a senior project manager and widely known as the brightest mind in the building. It was always a little embarrassing Monday morning when we'd come back to work talking about our weekend. Many of us did very little; movies, restaurants, or shopping. Ezzie read a novel, volunteered at a soup kitchen, and did a Tough Mudder 5K.

I remember asking her what she read last, and she said, "The Brethren – Inside the Supreme Court."

I was baffled and said, "The Brethren? Like for fun?"

Anyway, Ezzie was from the Dominican Republic and held two master's degrees, which was the *water cooler gossip* because the director only held a bachelor's degree. But she also had a great affinity for children. She came from a big family, and being a caretaker was just in her blood.

Her DC firm was bidding for a major development contract, but the front runner was clearly one of the big boys in DC. The director was trying everything possible to connect with the client's account manager but couldn't even get a return phone call.

Ezzie was not asked to assist in that development contract. She managed all her accounts flawlessly and also had another passion. She wanted the company to sponsor the county backpack drive for students. This was a countywide effort to supply students from underserved DC neighborhoods quality backpacks and school materials. She was constantly asking the director for the green light to support the county initiative, and finally, the director committed to a minor financial support.

Ezzie was thrilled, and that Saturday went to the chamber of commerce to announce their support. As she was waiting in the conference room, she met a representative from another organization supporting the backpack drive too. It turned out; it was the account manager for the contract they were bidding on. Long story short, the backpack drive was a great success, and because of Ezzie, her company got the development contract too.

If you think this is a story about coincidence or networking, I would argue differently. It was Ezzie's passion for children and supporting projects outside the normal realm of business. It was different. It was unique. That's the power of diversity and inclusion. It's new ideas. And because of those new ideas, it may open the door to new opportunities.

Two distinct criteria must be recognized by the leader to heighten the positive differences of your team. **Diversity** is awareness. **Inclusion** is the action. Both are necessary to gain greater influence and connection with your team. The payoff is a team that is productive, creative, aligned, and committed to you as a leader and the organization.

> *"To be trusted is a greater compliment than being loved."*
>
> *-George MacDonald*

## Chapter 9
# It's a Matter of Trust

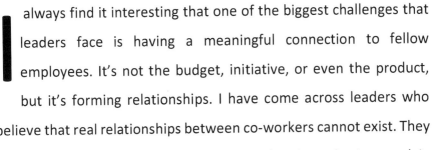

I always find it interesting that one of the biggest challenges that leaders face is having a meaningful connection to fellow employees. It's not the budget, initiative, or even the product, but it's forming relationships. I have come across leaders who believe that real relationships between co-workers cannot exist. They believe in the relationships between husbands and wives and in relationships between parents and children, but not relationships between co-workers. They think that co-workers are just people they work with. If you're in that camp, I've got news for you...you have a relationship with your fellow employees, too; and it's a work-based relationship.

n. Relationship: the way in which two or more people are connected, or the state of being connected.

One of the barometers to measure employee engagement and overall happiness at work is how relationships between colleagues are developing. The single biggest indicator of a healthy developing relationship is **Trust**. To *be the light* in your organization, garnering trust is mandatory. Ask yourself, what is the level of trust in your organization? How do you think your employees would answer that question? Consider the average make-up of an organization.

- Frontline/Associates
- Supervisors/Assistant Manager
- Manager/Senior Manager
- Director
- VP & C-Suite

Try to put yourself in your employee's shoes. Depending on where they work and who they report to, they may have completely different experiences in your organization. All leaders must actively seek and work toward trust. Trust is not given, it's earned. More importantly, it takes time to grow. According to recent studies, the level of trust in organizations are reaching all-time lows.

The American Psychological Association's *Work & Well-Being* Survey says:

- Only one in five employees says they trust their employer.

- Only half surveyed believe that their employers are open and upfront with them.

- One in three says their leaders are not honest.

Fostering trust between the employee and the leader is of utmost importance because that motivates them to put their best foot forward, be on good terms with their supervisor, and also spread positive word-of-mouth about the organization that they work for, attracting more talent. Employees are twice as more likely to experience workplace stress when they are unable to trust their employer. The likelihood of these employees going out to search for a new job is four times more.

In my young career, I landed a senior management position at a highly respected government contractor in Northern Virginia. The CEO attended a conference where I gave the keynote speech. Immediately after my speech, he reached out to me about working for him. We spoke on and off over the next 18 months, and with each conversation, he offered me an increase in my starting salary. I thought very highly of him, and I was definitely intrigued by the possibility.

Finally, he took me to lunch and offered me an incredible opportunity that was hard to resist -senior manager with security clearance, the highest salary I'd ever had, full benefits, and an office with a window. I was thrilled to say yes. That Friday afternoon, I attended a two-hour orientation and administrative day. This was my first red flag. The CEO was not at my orientation (which I hadn't expected), but the director in charge of the orientation had no idea who I was, and so she treated me like a *throwaway employee.* Her exact words were, "I don't know who you are, but I guess you're the fresh meat."

I laughed awkwardly, not knowing if she was joking or not. I dismissed the uncomfortable orientation and got ready for my first day. Monday morning, I arrived bright and early. The ten-floor building stood tall and was a staple in the city. I made my way through the crowded lobby and jumped on the elevator. It was interesting to watch different employees get on and off the elevator as I made my way up to the tenth floor. I got off the elevator and entered my new department. This encounter was my second red flag. I walked up to the young lady behind the front desk and introduced myself.

"Hi, my name is Darryl Ross. This is my first day."

She gave me a questioning look and said, "Do you have a badge?"

I smiled and said, "No, I attended the orientation last Friday, should I have gotten a badge then?"

She didn't respond. She just got on the phone and said to the other person on the line, "You have a new hire here!" Then she hung up the phone, looked at me and said, "He'll be out in a minute."

I said, "Okay, thank you." In my mind, I thought that wasn't the warmest of greetings. However, I quickly shook it off, knowing the CEO would greet me any minute.

About five minutes later, the door opened, and a gentleman said, "I'm Mike, follow me." It turned out that Mike was the COO and my direct report. He was not very friendly and seemed put off that I was even there. He quickly walked me into the conference room and dropped the hammer. He said, "You are being assigned 32 accounts. I want you to work with Chris. Learn all you can. These are formerly Chris's accounts. Chris doesn't know it yet, but we're letting him go after you're up to speed. Obviously, that is not public information. Your office is at the end of the hall. Go get settled in." And he walked out.

I sat there in disbelief. *What just happened? How did I get roped into this? And, where is the CEO?* I went into my office and started setting up. I stood there staring out the window, trying to process that meeting with the COO.

I heard a light knock on my door and in walked Chris. He said, "You must be the guy who is here to take my job." I was in shock. He said, "Don't worry about it. They don't think I know, but I do. You want some advice, run!" He began to tell me story after story of the company lying to clients and even fellow employees.

I tried to tell myself, "This is a disgruntled employee. Keep an open mind." But I was sick to my stomach. The entire situation felt wrong. Finally, I got to speak with the CEO around noon. I went into his office, closed the door, and spilled my guts. I shared my immediate thoughts on everything: orientation, the front desk girl, the COO, and Chris. I said, "You want the guy you're firing to be my trainer?"

The CEO tried to reassure me that they wanted me there. He said, "You are the positive difference we want in this organization. It will just take some time." He continued, "Chris has been a problem child from the very beginning. Before you know it, he'll be gone. You can drive those existing accounts and add new ones."

I nodded reluctantly, but I didn't tell him that Chris knew he was going to be fired. I figured it would cause me more of a problem. I decided to ignore my gut and move forward. I started meeting the clients and building up my accounts.

Chris was helpful on the account management but had daily negative comments. His usual was, "Well, at least these greedy jerks will have to pay me a severance package!"

Even though Chris had a negative attitude, part of me thought, *how can I blame him?* He knows he's going to be fired and he's training the guy who's replacing him. The whole thing was just odd.

By the end of the fourth week, I had a moment of clarity. I was in the break room alone when the CEO and COO walked in. They seemed to be half laughing and joking around. They definitely saw me sitting there but continued to talk out loud. I was surprised to hear that the two of them had something negative to say about half of the department. They went from name to name, saying words like *useless*, *overpaid*, and *arrogant*. It sounded like they disliked everyone. I couldn't believe that. Was I so naïve to think that they wouldn't speak poorly about me when I wasn't around too? So, I finally realized the problem. It was clear as a bell. I didn't trust them.

I resigned that day. I actually ended up leaving the company before Chris. Rumor has it, Chris left three days later.

I think back on that story and know that it was a bit extreme. I wouldn't want anyone to go through such an ordeal. But the major learning point was palpable. Yes, they could have been friendlier, especially to a new employee. But that wasn't the deal-breaker. It was a lack of trust. No amount of money, benefits, or office window could overcome the dysfunction of trust this company portrayed. So, how can you be sure the feeling of trust is alive and well in your organization? Take a trust audit.

- Are you constantly witnessing organizational issues? Be mindful. Organizational issues often trust issues in disguise. The employee frustration that is building up might just be a reaction to the uncertainty and lack of trust.

**Best Practice:** Listen to their concerns. Allow a forum for genuine feedback. Some of the frustration is a result of not being recognized and heard.

- Is your organization going through major changes? It's natural for employees to feel insecure during a change. This insecurity can morph into feelings of distrust.

**Best Practice:** Over-communicate and clarify perceptions. The more leadership can communicate, the more likely employees will feel there is genuine concern for them, which translates into trust.

- Employees have ears too. They know the rumors of layoff, acquisition, or new staff being hired.

**Best Practice:** Use WIIFM, which stands for *"What's in it for me."* When communicating with employees, shape the message to state clearly how it affects them directly. The leader who informs and is more transparent will continue to garner trust.

As in any relationship, trust is one of the most important factors for health outcomes. Leaders are tasked to balance the demands of the department, with a firm yet professional and authentic truth. From leadership in the C-suite to the frontline, trust is an evolving belief and reliability that all employees need to be productive and succeed.

*"One of the great challenges in this world is knowing enough about a subject to think you're right, but not enough about the subject to know you're wrong."*

*-Neil deGrasse Tyson*

*"The purpose of life is to contribute in some way to making things better."*

*-Robert F. Kennedy*

## Chapter 10
## The Light of Purpose

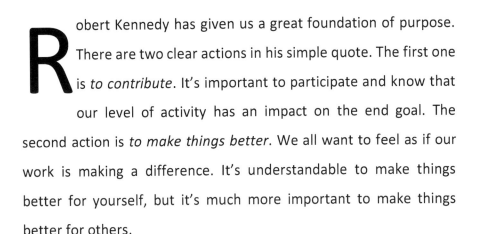

Robert Kennedy has given us a great foundation of purpose. There are two clear actions in his simple quote. The first one is *to contribute*. It's important to participate and know that our level of activity has an impact on the end goal. The second action is *to make things better*. We all want to feel as if our work is making a difference. It's understandable to make things better for yourself, but it's much more important to make things better for others.

*'A Theory of Human Motivation,'* was a paper in which Abraham Maslow introduced Maslow's hierarchy of needs, back in 1943. It was a significant study that identified what he thought was the main human drivers. In his work, he highlighted basic needs, physiological needs, and self-fulfillment needs. It was clear that contribution and *making a difference* are embodied in our self-fulfillment needs.

*'Being the light'* means having an awareness of our self-fulfillment needs and aligning them with our purpose. However, there is often one slight problem. Many leaders don't even know their purpose. Sometimes, leaders feel like they are literally working for a paycheck. What's worse, they can sense that their team may have the exact same feeling. How can leaders change their mindset to be more purpose-driven for themselves and their teams?

- Use the acronym B.E.S.T.
- **B**e Intentional
- **E**mpower the Meaning
- **S**erve & Support
- **T**ransform

## Be Intentional

Have you ever noticed the safety speech on an airplane? Specifically, the section on oxygen masks? The flight attendants say some variation of *"Should the cabin lose pressure; oxygen masks will drop from the overhead area. Please place the mask over your own mouth and nose before assisting others."*

Why do they say to place the mask on yourself first, before assisting others? Simple, you can't help others if you first haven't helped yourself. It's the same thing when it comes to discovering your purpose. Long before you assist your team members in finding their purpose, leaders must discover and fulfill their own purpose. Be intentional on your journey to fulfillment. Change your mindset and lean into the possibilities that your personal joy and happiness are a priority. Regardless of your role, seek opportunities that bring you closer to the discovery and art of fulfillment.

Also, don't forget to be intentional about positivity. Sometimes, the negativity in your office weighs you down. It's impossible to find your purpose if you're miserable. Many days you come to work, letting the ebbs and flows of the day dictate your level of positivity. Have you ever come to work in a good mood? You get great sleep, commute traffic is reasonable, and you feel positive. Then you walk into chaos. The negativity swarms you, and thirty minutes later, you're in a downward spiral of negativity. Take a moment for yourself. Breathe. Remember, your personal joy and happiness is a priority.

My dear friend is the HR Director for a hotel chain in Clearwater, Florida. She has a standup plaque on her desk that says, "No negativity allowed here!" If you walk in her office with the wrong energy, she will literally point at the plaque. It's hilarious because she's intentional about positivity. My personal favorite is a sign she has on her wall that says, "Sometimes the best part of my day is that my chair spins!" I love it. It's her reminder that her joy and happiness is a priority. You cannot ruin it.

However, I understand that sometimes there are major situations at work that require your serious attention and focus. But even a serious situation does not mean you are forced to be negative. It simply means to stay professional and compliant. On the other hand, the overly positive employee in a very serious situation can be annoying. Shortly after your company has some unfortunate employee layoffs, the *obnoxiously positive* employee walks in and says, "Hey guys, let's take our lemons and make lemonade!" That's just too much. They need to learn timing.

The good news is that there are many psychological and physiological benefits to positivity.

- A lower rate of depression
- A lower level of stress
- Higher resistance to the common cold

Here are two direct takeaways.

- Positivity puts the power back in your hands on how you're going to react every day.

- Positivity gives you a great balance and perspective, which is the doorway to your purpose.

*"We don't get to choose what happens to us, but we always get to choose how we react to it."*

**—G.S. Jennsen**

In the book, *Man's Search for Meaning*, Viktor Frankl chronicled how he spent his years in prison in the concentration camps of the Nazi's during World War II. Through all the torture and heartbreak, he still said, *"The last of human freedoms is the ability to choose one's own attitude."*

To discover your purpose, choose to live and work in an upbeat, happy environment. Be intentional about positivity.

## Empower the Meaning

To have a purpose, employees must have meaning in their work. Your role and everyday job tasks are important to the organization, but your purpose is a higher calling. One of my most memorable keynote speeches was the one I gave for the Prince William County Professional Development Day. This was an entire day dedicated to motivating all of the people who work in education: teachers, counselors, janitorial staff, security, bus drivers, facilities, and even food services.

A very polite, older gentleman named Sam walked up to me after my speech to say hello. I asked him what he does for Prince William County.

He said, "I'm part of the education team."

I smiled and said, "You're absolutely right. How do you do that?"

He said, "By transporting fresh food to the school cafeteria."

He understood the power of meaning. His job task was to pick up food, pack his van, and take the food to the school. But his purpose was to provide healthy fruits and vegetables to the students, so they had proper nourishment, which made them better students. Indeed, Sam was part of the education team.

I was introduced to *empowering the meaning* from my former sales job with Wyndham vacation resorts. Every day, the marketing department would provide customers, willing to listen to a 90-minute presentation on Timeshare. Of course, they were lured into this sales pitch by getting free tickets to a show on the Las Vegas strip. In other words, most of our customers had zero interest in getting a

Timeshare. They only wanted to show tickets. It was our job to change their mind and make the sale...that day.

When I started my career in Timeshare sales, I was very weak. After the first month, out of 50 sales representatives, I was the 47th— third from the bottom. I had a difficult time convincing people to pull out a credit card and buy a Timeshare package, which on average, costs $25,000 in 90 minutes. Then a shift happened in my mindset, which correlated to a boost in my performance. The shift was simple. Our VP, Gary Thien, saw my potential and helped give me meaning behind what I was doing.

He asked me, "How do you think it feels to vacation in one of our beautiful resorts with your family?"

Honestly, I didn't know. So, I purchased a small *employee rate*, tester vacation package for my family. This was a starter package that gave me limited vacation points, but perfect for a trial experience. I took my wife and two-year-old son to Oceanside, San Diego, for a weekend getaway using my Wyndham points. We stayed in a gold crown resort right on the beach. My fondest memory is a picture that my wife took of me holding my son on our hotel balcony. He was pointing at the ocean. This was his first time he ever saw the ocean in real life. He could see the waves crashing and smell the salt in the air. It was such a thrill as a parent.

At that moment, I could hear my VP's voice, *"How do you think it feels to vacation in one of our beautiful resorts with your family?"*

I had my answer; *it was amazing.* I realized I could never have afforded to stay on the beach in Oceanside San Diego unless I had a vacation package through Wyndham. It became crystal clear. My job task was to sell Timeshare, but my purpose was to help our guests create family memories. I immediately changed my entire approach to the sales presentation. I presented the opportunity to be a Wyndham vacation owner through the lens of my son. I'm proud to say that I went from the 47th sales rep to number one on our sales board, which landed me a promotion to be a specialist presenter.

Whether you are a new employee or a veteran, it's important for leaders to help team members see their value and empower them with the meaning behind their job tasks.

## Serve & Support

Never underestimate the power of serving and supporting your employees' purpose. When possible, assist team members in fostering a side project. Yes, they will need to complete their main duties, but help them develop their passion within the structure of the organization.

In a previous role, I was the VP of a patient experience training firm. Along with my daily duties, I remember wanting to develop an online video training platform. Before joining the firm, their online presence was very minimal. But with the approval of the CEO, my colleagues and I helped to develop a bi-weekly video training session that was provided as free content to our clients. In just a few short months, we had a substantial library of video training online. This was beneficial to the organization and, more importantly, extremely valuable to me in pursuing my purpose.

Another example of side-projects comes from the world of banking. I met a branch manager of a well-known bank in Tampa, Florida. He was passionate about training on financial literacy, specifically to his Latin speaking community. His bank supported him in going out to give free workshops on financial wellness. In return, he received a little bonus for each new person from one of his workshops who opened an account. Because the bank was open to the branch manager giving workshops, it fulfilled the branch manager's passion for training, while providing an additional stream of customers for the bank. That's a *win-win*!

Serving & supporting your team also means helping to grow the skill set of your employees. Ask yourself this question: *How much am I doing to develop the potential greatness in my team?* Take pride that they are willing to manage an additional project. Inquire about their progress. It's empowering for employees to know that you care and are genuinely pulling for them. Have them bounce ideas off you and provide some suggestions. This can potentially push them through mental roadblocks and give them momentum.

## Transform

As a leader, transform the mindset of your employees starting from day one with new employee orientation. For all your seasoned employees, create a re-boot orientation. In this meeting, you can reset and transform the organizational vision. Share how important it is for each team member to find their meaning and purpose in the organization.

Highlight two areas:

- **Organizational Ownership**: The organization needs to tell stories. Share your impact on customers and fellow employees on a larger scale. Take this seriously. Great things are happening every day in your organization, but the news doesn't spread. Be certain that purpose-driven stories are dominating the company's communication feed.

- **Employee Ownership:** Instill in the employees that they have skin in the game too. If approved, share that the leadership is open to new contributions. Employees can and should seek opportunities to go above and beyond. With the approval of their direct supervisor, employees can look to foster side projects within their existing accountabilities. This can definitely benefit the organization, but the actual purpose is to help the employee find deeper meaning in their work.

By bringing these two areas together, you are transforming the mindset and vision of your organization and heading to the path of purpose.

To *Be the Light* means much more than smiling at co-workers and customers. It's more than just being positive. It means in every encounter; your positive projection illuminates through guest excellence, communication, leadership, teambuilding, conflict, resilience, diversity, trust, and even your purpose. It's the intentional positive energy of your co-workers and customers that creates a company culture of kindness.

Now it's time to permit yourself to *be the light* every day. Train your employees and expect positivity from your department. We have let negativity hijack our day-to-day tasks. Let's take it back. *Be the light* for yourself, your team, your department, and your organization. **Be the Light!**

---

*For God has not given me a spirit of fear,
but of power and love and sound mind.*

**2 Timothy 1:7**

Listen and Subscribe to Darryl's Podcast: **Unity Works!**

In this podcast, Darryl shares positive insight on today's topical and sometimes controversial topics. He shapes the discussion through the lens of unity and acceptance while focusing on our community, families, and workplace. Life works better when we come together!

Found on: Apple Podcasts, Spotify, and iHeart Radio
For Speaking Engagements, inquire:
Keynote Speeches, Workshops, Webinars
Darryl Ross, Inc.
www.darrylrosslive.com
Email: darryl@darrylrosslive.com

## Meeting Planners & Event Coordinators

Energize your group. Darryl helps organizations and employees **like yours** get motivated and empowered to achieve more. Straight from the news desk, Darryl Ross is a former Fox 5 news reporter and currently one of the most requested motivational trainers. He's truly an entertainer at heart with a passion for people and service. His dynamic and high-energy presentation style makes him a favorite for corporations, associations, and healthcare organizations.

Darryl has appeared on numerous television networks, including *E! Entertainment*, *PBS*, and the *Travel Channel*. He shares proven success principles, motivation, leadership, and real-world strategies in his uniquely entertaining style. He will inspire your group to realize their potential. He is also author to the youth book, *Be Extraordinary: The Teenagers Roadmap to Success!*

Past clients include Mercedes Benz, World of Coca-Cola, Motorola, KedPlasma, University of Florida, and the Human Resources Association of Southern Maryland.

## WHAT THEY ARE SAYING...

Darryl did an outstanding presentation. My company is undergoing a lot of changes this year. He delivered a humorous perspective on managing change. He gave employees new ways to look at and deal with change. I even heard people talking about his presentation days after his visit. His presentation definitely motivates people to alter how they perceive and react to change. I personally did.

**Denise Reyes -Director of Human Resources Loudoun Water**

Darryl was the perfect speaker after a dull stockholders meeting. He was able to tailor his topics to fit matters relevant to our company. He was also very professional and had a good grasp of management issues. Additionally, and perhaps most importantly, his use of humor helped keep everyone's attention and made the evening enjoyable.

**Keith Appenzeller - CEO of King Engineering Associates, Inc.**

Darryl was wonderful. We worked together before the event so that he could learn a little about our company and our leadership's motivation needs. It is obvious that he did his research before the event as he spoke about our stores and our business. He was extremely professional, energetic, and knowledgeable about the topic. Our leaders loved how engaging and approachable he was. We wanted the session to last all day. I have had employees contacting me all day via email or by just stopping me in the hall to share with me how much they enjoyed his session. I highly recommend Darryl Ross!

**Sheri Kell - Human Resources Badcock Furniture**

\* \* \* \* \*

**Dear Darryl,**

On behalf of over 1,100 PWCS employees and especially myself, I would like to thank you for doing such an outstanding job as our Classified Professional Development Conference keynote speaker. Your presentation exceeded our expectations, and we were especially impressed by your unique energy, humor, and engaging delivery. We were all also greatly inspired by your message. It was a great way to begin our day and get our conference participants energized for the other sessions and training. Thank you for being a part of the success of our conference. We hope that you will visit us again.

**Kelli Stenhouse,**
**M.Ed. Department of Human Resources Prince William County**

# NOTES

*To, Raymond & Brenda Ross*
*All I am...is because of you!*